W9-CZH-556

The Actualist Anthology

photos — bottom left: Dom Franco; the others: Morty Sklar
people (from top left, counterclockwise): 1) John Sjoberg, 2) Pat Casteel & Jim Mulac,
3) Dave Morice, 4) Pat Casteel, Dave Morice, Chuck Miller, 5) Barbara Sablove, Pat
Dooley, Steve Toth's arm.

The Actualist Anthology

edited by

MORTY SKLAR & DARRELL GRAY

for subscribers to
The Spirit That Moves Us magazine
this book is offered as Volume 2, Numbers 2&3

Cover design & illustration by Pat Dooley
Typography, design & layout of contents by Morty
Sklar, as well as all photos except one on
page 1 and those on pages 14, 35, 55,
68 & 93 (credited there).

The Spirit That Moves Us Press
Morty Sklar/P.O. Box 1585
Iowa City, Iowa 52240/(319) 338-5569

The Spirit That Moves Us Press is a non-profit, IRS tax-exempt organization (donations are tax-deductible) which publishes the literary periodical of the same name, and books. **In Fall 1977** we'll be again sponsoring, with partial assistance from the Iowa Arts Council, **Poetry-In-The-Buses**—this time with drawings (announcements will be made; meanwhile please include a self-addressed, stamped envelope with enquiries—*for this and everything*). **We're also setting up** racks of non-commercial literary periodicals in Iowa City & Sioux City, as well as in bookstores. **We continue to sponsor** free readings. **Manuscripts of poetry** (no book-length) are welcome—with *self-addressed, stamped envelopes.*

Items listed on pages 8 & 9 may be ordered from

The Spirit That Moves Us Press

Morty Sklar/P.O. Box 1585
Iowa City, Iowa 52240/(319) 338-5569

or

from *Plains Distribution; Truck Distribution; CCLM Library Sub-scription Service; Energy BlackSouth; Skylo; EBSCO, Faxon, Macgregor, & The Instructor* subscription agencies; COSMEP *Book Bus.* The magazine is available on **Microfilm** from Gaylord Brothers.

We're listed in Bill Katz' 3rd edition of *Magazines for Libraries; Index of American Periodical Verse; Ulrich's; The Access Index to Little Magazines; The International Directory of Little Magazines & Small Presses; National Index of Literary Periodicals; MidAmerica V: A Bibliography of Midwestern Literature; Book Publishers of The United States and Canada* . . .

copyright © 1977 by The Spirit That Moves Us;
all rights revert to the contributors.

Not only, by law, may no part of this book be reproduced by any means (except for small portions for inclusion in reviews) without written permission of the publisher and contributors, but our actual continuance *depends on* people buying our stuff.

Library of Congress Cataloguing In Publication Data
Main entry under title:

The Actualist anthology

Includes bibliography and index
1. American poetry - Iowa City - Iowa   2. American poetry - 20th century
I. Sklar, Morty 1935 -   II. Gray, Darrell, 1945 -
PS572.I53A3   811'.5'408   77-81513
ISBN 0-930370-02-3   paper   ISBN 0-930370-03-1   cloth

Member: COSMEP; CCLM; Plains Distribution Service.

WELCOME!

Our original desire was to publish in one volume, the poets herein. Calling this volume THE ACTUALIST ANTHOLOGY came mainly out of a need for a title. "Fourteen Iowa City Poets" wouldn't have been accurate — this is *not* a regional anthology in a strict sense: we come from, among other places, New York City, Newton (Iowa), Hungary, Chicago, Finland, San Francisco, Saint Louis and even Iowa City!

(From "What Actually Is Actualism", an article by Morty in *Zahir* No. 9/Summer '77:) "What we have in common — 1) A basically open, generous and positive approach to our art. Maybe "positive" has connotations of Dale Carnegie or Norman Vincent Peale, so let's say "affirmative". So that even when bad times are central to a work, something inspiring/moving can occur . . . 2) Each Actualist is concerned with connecting with the reader on *some* level."

(From Darrell's new ESSAYS & DISSOLUTIONS from Abraxas Press:) "To be Actual is not to *possess* Actuality — it is to be possessed by it . . . I want to emphasize that Actualism is not an aesthetic "movement" in the usual sense of the word. It owes nothing to literary history that it could not find elsewhere, least of all aesthetic theory or literary criticism. Actualism begins when the Automorph in man's being decides to wake him up."

As with any anthology, there will be interest in why certain people are included and others not. Within the purview of this book we have sought to represent the work of those poets most seminal to the Actualist Movement, which began (in spirit, if not name) around 1970 in Iowa City, Iowa. Half of us remain in Iowa City, while others have moved to other parts of the country.

The word "Actualism" may strike the reader as just another ism, but in historical terms it is much more than that. It is a community, not always with similar interests, but always a community. The poet's sense of his/her writing becomes a part of that community.

Something we want to say before you do: Only two women are represented in this volume, and no Blacks, among other "categories" of people. That's because the anthology didn't seek out the poets in it—they were there.

Concerning the order in which the poets appear: In partial explanation, the book is conceived organically, with the poets thought of in proximity to one another—which in some cases puts one next to another much like him/her, or much *un*like. Or both. To cite an oddball example of the "organics" of this process, Dave Morice is last simply because his last poem seems a good last poem also for the anthology. Concerning the amount of pages per poet, we refer the reader to our two basic guidelines: 1) The best work (as *we* see it) we could find, combined with 2) The widest range.

What isn't in this volume, which we wanted to include but could not, due to our 144-page limit: 1) A special section for collaborative poems (of which there are hundreds & hundreds, written at parties, visits or wherever the spirit moved as many as four people to write a two-line poem, or as few as two to write a chapbook of 14 sonnets), 2) Photos of Actualist events, where not only poetry and fiction was read, but original plays and music performed, films shown, paintings displayed, and so on, 3) Representation of people who did much of the artwork for the Iowa City magazines *Search For Tomorrow; Gum; Suction; Dental Floss; P.F.Flyer; Me Too; Candy; Matchbook; Toothpaste; The Spirit That Moves Us*: Pat Dooley, Tim Hildebrand, Mary Ferris, David Sessions, Jane Miller, others — including some of the people in this anthology, 4) Reproductions of some of the magazine covers, and posters announcing readings and other events.

Whatever's left to say will best wait for Darrell's History of the Actualist Movement in the Arts — or something like that. Meanwhile, we all hope you'll enjoy this offering, and that somehow the spirit of the work will convey all that we want it to — and maybe even more!

Actually yours,

Morty Sklar & Darrell Gray
Iowa City & Berkeley, Summer 1977

THANKS

to Bob Thompson; Norm Sage; Kay
Chambers; Audrey Teeter for bringing Morty
to Iowa City; Iowa City for being so Great; Dom
Franco; the good times & the bad; our subscribers
and other supporters; COSMEP for helping us get
oriented in the real contemporary literature
world; The National Endowment for the Arts
for a grant in partial support of this
project; and to everyone else who,
at the writing of this didn't
come to mind, but you're there
somewhere, and you know who
you are.

This book is dedicated to the memory
of Jack Sklar (1897 – July, 1977) and to Selma Sklar,
and *all* our parents, both flesh & spiritual.

Also Available From
THE SPIRIT THAT MOVES US PRESS

The Spirit That Moves Us literary periodical (ISSN 0364-4014):
subscription: $3+75¢ postage/year to individuals; $5+75¢ postage to libraries

Volume 1, Number 1/Fall '75 — $1.50. Attila Jozsef, Michael Lally, Barbara Holland, Jack Marshall, Paul Violi, Rainer Maria Rilke, Cat Doty, Madeleine Keller, Nikolai Gumilev & 17 more; artwork all by Cat Doty

Volume 1, Number 2/Winter '75/'76 — $1.50. Charles Potts, Lyn Lifshin, John Batki, Jane Barnes, Big John Birkbeck, Dario Semper, Alice Kolb, & featuring Elizabeth Zima's howl-of-a 17-page poem with fine special drawings by David Sessions, plus 12 others

Volume 1, Number 3/Spring '76 — *rare* — but still available to patrons (donations of $25 or more). Anselm Hollo, Pablo Neruda, Rachel Hadas, Daniel Stokes, Christine Zawadiwsky, Lars Lundkvist, Tom Disch, Warren Woessner, Joan Colby, Fred Tarr, Sigrid Bergie, David Hilton & 22 others, with a special Pat Dooley cover

Volume 2, Number 1/Fall '76 — *rare* — but still available to patrons (donations of $25 or more). Tom Veitch, Hermann Hesse, Barbara Yates, Guy Beining, Carlos Reyes, Michael Hogan, Tom Montag, Joan Smith, Richard Kostelanetz, Clayton Eshleman, Glen Epstein, Jack Anderson, Freya Manfred, Jim Stephens & 18 others, with a special cover drawing by David Sessions.

Volume 2, Numbers 2&3/Winter&Spring '77; also known as THE ACTUALIST ANTHOLOGY (ISBN 0-930370-02-3 paper; ISBN 0-930370-03-1 cloth), edited by Morty Sklar & Darrell Gray; $3.50 perfect-bound (offered to subscribers as part of their subscriptions; $8 cloth; 144 pages with photos of the authors plus other photos, of Actualist events; and a special cover by Pat Dooley. Allan Kornblum, Chuck Miller, Anselm Hollo, Cinda Kornblum, Morty Sklar, John Batki, Darrell Gray, Jim Mulac, David Hilton, Sheila Heldenbrand, George Mattingly, John Sjoberg, Steve Toth, Dave Morice — seminal poets of the Actualist Movement.

"If *The Spirit That Moves Us* keeps moving the way it has been, it should move itself up among the most valuable and lasting magazines of poetry."
— *Small Press Review*

RIVERSIDE (ISBN 0-930370-00-7), by Morty Sklar; 1974; handset in Bembo and handprinted on Ragston; photo cover (screened zinc cut); handsewn; 150 copies; $2.25

THE POEM YOU ASKED FOR (ISBN 0-930370-01-5), by Marianne Wolfe; 1977; composed in Baskerville and printed photo offset with an original drawing by Elizabeth Pickard-Ginsberg for the two-color cover; $1.00 ("You want to read each poem again. And you do; you will." —*Joan Smith*)

THE ACTUALIST ANTHOLOGY (ISBN 0-930370-02-3 paper; ISBN 0-930370-03-1 cloth)(also known as Volume 2, Numbers 2&3 of *The Spirit That Moves Us* magazine)(ISSN 0364-4014), edited by Morty Sklar & Darrell Gray; 1977; composed in Baskerville and printed photo offset on ivory paper with 3-color cover drawing by Pat Dooley; photos of the poets,and other photos (see opposite page, **Volume 2, Numbers 2&3** for names of poets). $3.50 perfectbound (but *offered to subscribers as part of their subscriptions!*); $8 cloth; 144 pages

THE NIGHT WE STOOD UP FOR OUR RIGHTS: Poems 1969-1975, by Morty Sklar (published by Toothpaste Press; ISBN 0-915124-11-4 paper; ISBN 0-915124-12-2 cloth); 1977; composed in Perpetua & printed on Strathmore Beau Brilliant, letterpress; 650 copies smyth sewn & glued into wrappers, & 50 signed copies quarter bound in cloth and handmade Moetachi paper; original cover drawing by James Harrison; $4 paper

THE FIRST POEM, by Morty Sklar (published by Snapper Press); 1977; handset in Helvetica & Mistral and handprinted; original drawing/zinc cut cover by David Sessions; 250 copies; $2.25

BROADSIDE SAMPLER FROM THE ACTUALIST ANTHOLOGY ; 3 colors with several poems printed over the anthology's cover drawing on 11x14 heavy stock; $1.00

POETRY-WITH-DRAWINGS IN THE BUSES 1977/78; from poems selected from submissions from anywhere, and drawings made especially for each of the eight; composed in several typefaces & printed on variously colored heavy 11x14 stock for placement in buses, *but of course, may be placed anywhere*... a small brochure with reproductions of the placards will be available at the beginning of the year for 50¢... the placards themselves, $1.00 but the complete set of 8 plus an info placard, only $6 ... discounts for bus companies, arts councils or others ordering in quantity.

12

Steve Toth

Dave Morice

Allan Kornblum

photo by T.L. Gettings

Born, 1949 in Beth Israel Hospital in New York City. Parents: Seymour Kornblum, social worker; Anne Epstein Kornblum, elementary school teacher.

Education: Pierre S. du Pont High School, Wilmington, Delaware, grad '67. One semester as voice ed. major at N.Y.U. One year at St. Marks Poetry Project Workshops. Three semesters as an English major at U. of Iowa.

Work experience: paper boy, magazine salesman, shipping clerk in storm window factory & in a clothing factory, indoor & outdoor janitor, busboy, usher at the Fillmore East, flower shop clerk, assembly-line in a shoe factory, etc.

Current occupation: part-time teacher, small-job printer, printer & co-publisher of Toothpaste Press poetry books, and poet.

Important moments: Being born to two Jewish left-wing idealists. Watching a 2-part tv show about Sacco & Vanzetti with my parents sometime during childhood. World Fellowship summer camp, c. '58. First guitar, c. Autumn '58. Singing under Robert Page at the Delaware Music Camp, '62. Sol Kutner's buying me a record player, same summer. Good high school English & drama teachers. Chancing on a T.S. Eliot record in the Wilmington Library. N.Y.U. friends, Kelley, Miguel, Mark, George, Dan, Fred & Nancy, Miles & Carmella, even Carl, and now dead — John & Rod. Hearing Ted Berrigan read, December 1967. Burning my draft card, c. January, '68. Living with Mary for 6 months in '69. St. Marks workshops, Oct. '69 — June '70. Moving to Iowa City July 3, 1970. Meeting, then living with Cinda Wormley shortly thereafter. Starting Toothpaste magazine . . . first issue, August '70. Meeting and growing to love all the Iowa City Actualists, and becoming part of a community-of-the-spirit. Taking Harry Duncan's typography class September '70, and meeting Iowa City printers, Al Buck, Tom Miller, Howie & Kay, Kim Merker, & John G. Henry. Buying our first printing press, April 1972. Getting married with Cinda, and moving to West Branch August '72.

Thanks to my poetry teachers in workshops: Dick Gallup, Carter Radcliff, Tom Veitch, Ted Berrigan, Jack Marshall, Donald Justice, and Anselm Hollo.

And thanks to all the writers in this anthology, and the many other people I've known and loved these last seven years in Iowa.

Some of these poems have appeared in the magazines *Painted Bride Quarterly; New York Times; The Sou'wester; Out There; Suction; Wild Onions; Search For Tomorrow; Gum; The Spirit That Moves Us*, and the following books, except the first and third ones.

Books:

FAMOUS AMERICANS, self-published; 1970 (o.p.)

TIGHT PANTS, self-published; 1972 (o.p.)

GOOD MORNING: 14 SONNETS (with Darrell Gray), J. Stone Press Weekly, 5399½ Bryant, Oakland, California 94618; 1975

THE SALAD BUSHES, Seamark Press, Box 2, Iowa City, Iowa 52240; 1975

THRESHOLD, The Toothpaste Press, Box 546, West Branch, Iowa 52358; 1976

HER HAIR IS WET

And behold the bee of sleep
At the umbrella's tip
　　　　　　　　—Reverdy

The soft lips of the heat register
Open, breathe, and above it particles of air
Solidify into furniture.
For no reason, you feel as if you should
Know the young girl in the zebra striped coat
Sitting on the newly formed and hovering davenport
And you start to say . . . .
But she interrupts. My hair is wet, I hope
The plush of this divan isn't being ruined
I'd best walk around
I came in to get out of the rain.
You take her hand and lead her into the yellow kitchen.
Taffeta curtains are stuffed in a vase on the table
Violets and grapes frame the windows
With the beginning and end of summer
Il pleut, she turns from the window eating a grape
Il pleut, she says again
And takes the memory of coffee you offer

THE TRUCKERS

Move objects we desire
Closer to us
Almost 'within' our grasp
Like love which we know can't
Be held or bought
Yet we can smell
Yet can the wheels

Support the weight of what's in back,
Of our minds, a sandwich
Perked up by the crisp vegetables
Living dreams that wouldn't crunch
If they weren't fresh
The driver knows this
And cares about the miles

ALL THAT GLITTERS

There are limits to how long we live.
We are here because our parents were here.
Spring, summer, fall, winter, spring.
Sure aren't all that many great themes.
Iron rusts and silver tarnishes, but
all that glitters IS gold.
The bible tells me so.
The bible and Hegel, struggling from the
gloom of his books towards the kitchen
to see what the possibilities look like
from that angle.
Opening the window, he holds out a beer stein,
and an angel pees into it.
Drinking later with gusto, he wonders
why philosophy seems so pallid compared
to soccer on an autumn afternoon,
or Henry Ford's new factory in Detroit U.S.A.

AWKWARD SONG FOR MY SISTERS

Sometimes the flautist's hands
grasp the flute awkardly.

Now and then the dancer's body moves
into, then out of a clumsy position.

Occasionally the poet stutters,
lovers sit on the bed to a loud thump.

Often one corner of the coffin
slips while lowered into the grave,

and the lurch brings
another wave of tears.

Is there a more graceful
shape than a tear,

or a more unselfconsciously
awkward gesture than weeping?

Sometimes it rains for a week, then
surprise, the sun shines bright

and every object seems to have
hard edges...colors clash...

nothing seems to soften the awkward song.
But it continues like light,

like an arm around a shoulder,
the artist adds another shadow,

the flautist a trill,
the dancer a whirl,

and soon grass will grow
over our mother's grave..

3 DAYS AFTER FATHER'S DAY

for Seymour Kornblum and John Wormley

I'm sitting on the second floor of my house in West Branch
Iowa looking across the rolling fields at interstate 80.
To my left some 1,200 miles
My father is at his office, organizing the data for his
Ph.D. thesis, he is 53, living near Philadelphia,
Working in Philadelphia, proving
That happiness physically retards the aging process.
Much closer to my right, only about 100 miles west,
Cinda's father is doing whatever must be done
To make the corn and soybeans grow.
When we visit the Wormley farm we sleep in the corner
Of the room, the exact spot where he was born
'Watch out!' he jokes he knows about that kind of energy
Every year the corn and beans come up, a few new calves
He is a good German farmer.
I have been reading H. G. Wells'
OUTLINE OF HISTORY and Cinda and I are certainly part of
The Great Pattern — mixing racial stocks.
I am Semitic mixed with...no doubt some Russian or
Central Asian, Wells says there was a Central Asian tribe, the
Alans and there must be some psychic link, well, there might be.
And Cinda, Aryan plus probably in the past
A little from the Mongol tribes that swept through Europe
Her eyes are almost Oriental sometimes.
The Des Moines Sunday Register quotes Rabbi Heschel,
'But I would say to young people that in spite of the
negative qualities they may discover in their fathers,
they should remember that the most important thing
is to ponder the mystery of their own existence.'
The Des Moines Sunday Register also ponders the existence
of interstate 80, we humans are so impressed by physical
Things and Wells says the springtime human sacrifice

Spread throughout the world because it was impressive
Below my window is my first vegetable garden
I close my eyes and imagine a human sacrifice — it is impressive.
I open my eyes and there is interstate 80
I can see that 'occurrence' is spatially perceived.
That idea did not occur to me but when Darrell pointed it out
I flashed I laughed and said this is part of what makes living in
Iowa City worthwhile! and Dave and Cinda who were there
                                        too, agreed,
I said all the wheels in my head are turning and the wheels
On the cars are turning as they move from one side of my
                                        window
To the other and pass out of sight, East or West as Darrell's
Incredible diagrams showed, consciousness *is* outside space and
                                        time, i.e.,
Hello Dad, you here? have a beer
Hello John, you here? have a beer
We all want to be accepted, to be high,
Between these ideas and the world sometimes damn hard
To get up in the morning, sometimes so exciting
I never want to sleep, then I do sleep
In my house in West Branch Iowa with Cinda
With my father and mother with her father and mother
We all sleep together when we sleep

A LOT OF HEARTS ARE POUNDING IN THE UNIVERSE

When resentments seem to have
A reason
The fights begin.

On television the man doesn't
Know what to say to a man he loves,
His brother, and tells the nurse

"You're in love with him
You'll know what to say
When he wakes up"

Then he wakes up and runs out
So fast (to attend urgent unfinished business)
That no one gets a chance to...to get things straight.

A lot of hearts are pounding in the universe
And a conscious effort is made to
Make them relax

The way trumpets are part of
A conscious effort
To make us feel heroic.

Is this a mask or a clue
12 o'clock high
Now ending with a forced joke.

Outside steady lightning gives the clouds
A form I can hold in my eye...Ha
An angry sky, an angry heart

I feel as if I am a part of history...
I evade my life. "When and how will nature

Take revenge on the human race"...

Is that evasion
Or perspective
Floating mote of dust adrift etcetera.

When my friends piss me off,
I hear the Williams line, "What shall I say
For talk I must..."

But using words for an incident
Suddenly appears to be an assumption of
A responsibility to denude illusions

And just whose illusions are they?
Maybe mine.
O once again I long for my salad bushes

When will they bear fruit?
Perhaps in this country home
Photosynthesis will clear the air enough

For me to eat
Again with my friends
In peace.

IMMEDIATE KINDNESS

I had just found the bottle opener
when God walked in and
          spoke with a purple tongue

The pilgrimage for my contemporary

Canterbury Tales will be a fact-finding
      tour of the ubiquitous

war fronts of Southeast Asia. Victory
at Rummy 500! The bride wore white,
      her maids in blue, rented tuxedos

and a photographer moving the garbage cans
from my stoop to the bodega for a better
      picture, spieling in Spanish

about smiles. I held my Heinekens and
my guitar and waited for the flashes to
      finish. When I got upstairs

God walked in and spoke
with a purple tongue. He asked for a
      yellow steam shovel to move

things around, and an operator's manual.
I saw only his tongue, but I knew
      immediately that he was kind.

O LIGHT

    we understand
    how you show us
    to the door

    but how
    do you turn
    the handle?

SOMETHING PASSIONATE FOR CINDA

we are not the ones who are afraid of science
but neither are we the ones whom it aids
for i am still bored.
i wish a cyclone of love would whirl us away

like Pecos Bill, but not quite.
the structures of our lives might crush us
when the tornado tears trees and buildings
from their roots and foundations.

i wanted to write you a love poem
to tell you how beautiful were the leaves
in the trees outside, but i was too bored.
i wanted to do something physical

like chop the trees down, or like
delivering the mail, but not quite.
like listening to a recording of the breeze
in the yellow leaves of those trees.

no, a stereo recording of the sunset
accompanying a silent film of a pianist
playing his piano for an hour and a half.
science doesn't deliver our mail,

but at least we can talk about
the latest-developments-in-science.
we can't talk about the mail for long
before we're bored. now that i think of it

i wouldn't want to talk forever of science
either, neither would you. i'm blue.
i'm bored is what's the matter and i feel
as if i ought not to be as i'm in love with you

Chuck Miller

photo by Morty Sklar

"born and grew up in Midwest, parents were itinerant school teachers; gone to school for endless ages right up to the present a lot of conflicts with the bureaucracy sent to prison for a few years   lived in Europe for a short time and felt that to be very helpful   felt most interested in writers like Hesse, Remarque, Celine, Henry Miller, Kerouac, Bukowski, Pavese, Borchert. . . since there is little work for teachers or writers trying to figure out how and where to survive lately been thinking of what it means maybe to be a Midwestern writer with exemplars such as Meridel LeSeur and Sherwood Anderson and his Mid-America chants   and too that sense you get from Edgar Masters of the bitterness of life here, the straight forward beauty of it, and the crushing narrowness of it at the same time"

Some of these poems have appeared in the magazines *Suction; Free Flowing; The Spirit That Moves Us*, and the latter two books which follow.

Books:

A THOUSAND SMILING CRETINS, Friends Press; 1966
HOOKAH, by the author in cahoots with Seamark Press; 1971
OXIDES, Seamark Press, 722 Iowa Avenue, Iowa City, Iowa 52240; 1976

HOW IN THE MORNING

why always in the morning?
because you must begin your life over again each morning
you fumble for your shoes
the leather thongs stiff and cold
fumble with your fly
make sure your prick doesn't get caught in the zipper
and by then the shadows are stealing up grey and clean
the sun a later gamble
that might make it through this hung over sky
then the long walk out from the private shack of our dreams
barely holding together
to the car slowly disintegrating
if you can get it going
drive toward the world
only just functioning on the grey edge of night
with its slouched coffee slurpers
and unconscious donut gobblers
its shoe factories stitching on soles
for the tender feet of our souls
its bellowing trucks, posts and positions
sinecures, backbreaking sweats
being fed the slimy exhausts
of the constant velvet farts of our metal skins
sown onto us,
and it is all simple, grey, clear
if you don't think about it
there are those with their great life's works
and those who must do these very same great life's works
maybe Vallejo is riding with you this morning
looking for work the same as you
and he says "Understanding that he knows I love him,
that I hate him with affection
and to me he is in sum indifferent, I signal to him,
he comes, and I embrace him moved,

So What! Moved...Moved."
and I say to him "that was damn good Cesar
should we try the employment office today
or the toilet paper factory should we try
the donut factory once more to make that
graveyard donut shift, or maybe the mental hospital
to see if they have an opening in the laundry
I used to do the laundry thing folded sheets
off the mangle"
Cesar is saying
"go for the pop bottles, fuck all this other stuff
these wood bees, let's just collect pop bottles
that's the surest way"
and so the morning comes grey over the hills
you drop the washcloth on your cold feet
and fumble with the delicate
birds of morning
opening their cages

WHEN I BEGAN THIS FUNNY JOURNEY

when i began this funny journey
it was the pumping thuds
the heartbeat of prose
that i loved
the clear sonorous hoofbeats of meaning
the people there
laughing and weeping all over you
until you had them in your arms
and you fell down together
on the tavern floor
amidst the sawdust and sneering knees
the kicks and the bottles

now i am thirty
and i am beginning
to really love poems
i eat them for breakfast
i fuck them in my lonely bed
like lacey icing on cakes i eat them
like an Irish stew of the Mutter Sprached world
venison of strangeness
they are my walking stick
my overcoat

the poets are so good
because they don't say much
they are always saying less and less
leaving things out
turning into ghosts
they are endlessly beautifully
gibbering in my ear

but i dont eat dead poems

and more than this i prefer taking drugs
and even more than that i prefer love

but i think it will be an old tipsy poet
in a great shabby overcoat, yellow decaying
manuscripts trailing from his autumn pockets,
who will
some spectral midnight
come stumbling
after me

and laying his palsied hand
upon my trembling arm,

say, ever so softly
poetry is a vast muttering
of what you always knew it would be about

THE DUKE OF YORK (COURAGE)

death departs and i am drunk
on wine, on talk
we set sail again
through the needle's eye of the horizon
past the mists
stand at the bar and the yellow foam churns past our prows
mariners bound east
for the hanging gardens of Maya
"i have seen the white beaches in the sky"

bandy-legged boozers quaffing it down
with their mustachios and rakish dissolution
their sexes have traveled also extensively
now half stirring under tables
or shaping the jib of slacks
sad corporals in a defeated army
sallow lasses dressed like gay pirates
ships great busted figureheads
seeking a more myth-like, less found, port

then in the quiet wake of waves
the roar of talk and laughter abates
our animated gestures fall stuporous into dank lagoon
the primordial boozers stare of lost muddled helplessness
yet in back of that red eye still flash the lost continents
we might be a tavern full of old sea dogs
smuggled through the centuries
or any such bullshit half swashed dope runners story tellers
under the barmaids beer rag of our washed up fates
we're simple children
thinking of beds for the evening
and warm sexed creatures for nestling

FOR JUDY

in the West day is drawn into the smelter of sunset
each grain of light and all that it illumined
we might be out on the plain
weeping, protesting, crying out
this loss so utterly absolute

instead there is the subdued silence of dusk
lights in windows burn stoicly
with a sort of frail transcendence
as though an old woman
lifted unsteadily
her withered arm
for a last gesture at day

a lake of dark comes washing up
stars put forth pale blossoms

what i loved incinerated
in a smoldering weeping

a cry
so far
it is a wire scraping in the throat of childhood's distance
filament of innocence

there was a house
with a cheerful yellow light
a woman wet with luscious peace
with the dark of her meditating eyes
who waited in quiet half-lit rooms

who waits no longer
turns
and enters the smelter of night
the black factory

THING AS THEY ARE

going out halfhappy
or half angry or somewhat tired
nonetheless everything in this snow
looks back directly
with a stark clearness
as i walk through this nonessential winter's day
beautiful in a way which is neither grandiose
nor too little
all the elements have announced themselves
now they break and reform
in ways that are almost recognizable

tonight stars creak
like leather harnesses
alone in the solitude
of winter rooms
feel the harness of night around your back
and belly
the icy bit in your teeth
and be pulling it
alone in the dark
know there is no way out
or through, except the long strange road ahead
in which you are the uncertain captain
of this tramp steamer your life
various companions changing through the years
like stars in the same constellation
burning intensely but too far
in their fixed orbits
and the special ones
that come terribly close
the tail of a comet passing over
your trembling body
causing strange atmospheric disturbances

pulling out great gravitational hunks
finally always coming back to the same worn self
a cave glowing darker with experience
and less comprehensible in its depths

but in summer's first fragrance
still to break off bits of the milky way
and see the evening star
rising over the dark blue drifting up from the sunset
and rejoice as though you were young once more
and saw the dawn of hope rising just beyond your reach

I WRITE FOR THOSE UNKNOWN

i write for those unknown who were born unknown
who sat up in bed years later born again
and died unknown even to themselves
who could not know what i say
i write for Verlaine still praying the pietas
in his cell in Belgium
i write because i cannot sleep for having visions
for Van Gogh who splashes my wall with joy
and who painted absolute reality
i understood this and was unalterably changed
i write because i return to my bed at night
like a convict to his cell
i write because i have given up all hope
and do not even know what i say
i write for no reason at all
because time is running out
and nothing ever changes
i write because there is a vast commune
spread over the earth
and we are all touching hands in the mist

laughing gently and with compassion
i write because nothing comes back
and i have lost treasures of the wildest imaginings
i write because i am chewing the last rag of solitude
and still find a kind of delirious nourishment there
i write because when i opened my pipes
out came a pineapple made of pain
i write to have my 2 cents worth of erratic song
and be a part of the collective madness
i write because i am soon to sleep
and will rise tomorrow
to hawk my bones on the streets
just as you in your turn
will stumble half conscious
from your hovel
we will bump clumsily into one another
step back squinteyed and suspicious
not recognizing nor understanding
go our blinded ways

REQUIEM: A SURREALIST GRAVEYARD

there was Nadja's glove flickering somewhere
under the Madza bulb
which i think of now and then
an imaginary semi-transparent thing lost somehow
in what we could call a quantum of our love
a space-time geometry with its coordinate seam
unzipped onto the void,
does the void collect our mad love
surely the only kind which could exist
like a soft blue grave yard
upsidedown in a telescope eye

clasping us with the love of its ether arms
poor Mickelson-Morley trying to prove ether love with mirrors,
mirrors we can only disappear into with Huertibus
their love too fathomless for our mortal dimensions
but the ether wind spills down sometimes
wetting our seared black cheeks
and we realize it must be the kindly blue grave yard,
or is someone basting the earth in silence?
a great baked apple stewing in space
the gigantic spoon up-lifted
i hear silence running over the curve of the sky
but there is something i have lost
which we all wore then, remember comrades?
the good luck glove
i have lost the good luck glove
it kept me going in this rain of sad asteroids
i have lost the good luck glove
my hand like a socket in space
wanders already on that journey to another star

Anselm Hollo

photo by Sunpapers: Clarence B. Garrett

"Anselm Hollo was born in Helsinki, Finland, in 1934: first came to the U.S. in 1951, his senior year in high school (McKinley High, Cedar Rapids, Iowa). Subsequently, he lived & worked in Germany, Austria, Spain, and London, England (8½ years with the BBC). Since 1967, he has taught at various colleges & universities in this country: SUNY at Buffalo, U. of Iowa in Iowa City, Bowling Green State, Michigan State, Hobart & Wm. Smith, etc. He is glad to be a small vortex in a tradition that goes back to the Mayan Codices & forward to infinity (maybe)."

These poems appear in many magazines and in the following books *except* the first and last, with most in the next-to-last.

Books:

SENSATION 27, The Institute of Further Studies (o.p.)
MOTES, Joujouka Toujours (author's imprint) (o.p.)
MAYA, Cape Goliard Press (defunct) (o.p.)
SOJOURNER MICROCOSMS: New & Selected Poems 1959-77, Blue Wind Press, 820 Miramar, Berkeley, Calif. 94707; forthcoming 1977
HEAVY JARS, The Toothpaste Press, Box 546, West Branch, Iowa 52358; forthcoming 1977

SONG OF THE TUSK

the elephant
      bogged down
thousands of years ago

the fragmentary tusk
      now in a glass case

no no those are untrue statements
it is I
      am in the glass case
            counting
                  the stubs of museum tickets

it is the elephant
      walks the downs
            laughs at the sea
                  growling

there is no such thing
      as thousands of years
I drop a stone on your head
      from the elephant's back

show me
      show me the thousands of years

I walk through the water
      throwing stones at the women
            on the beach
            the honeymoon women
                  their eyes far apart

frightened
      they close the glass case

over themselves & their lovers
for thousands of years

A WARRANT IS OUT FOR THE ARREST OF HENRY MILLER

(November 2, 1962)

get that man!
what rooftop
chases!   zig-
zag sprints in alleys
smelling of garlic
& good fucks
get that man!
he's alive...

skittering
down fire escapes,
the women watching
with big startled tits
rock-drill roar
& torch flash
down into fall-
out shelters —

but all the while he sits on a mountaintop
& smiles at sparrows hatching
at the foot of the ladder to man's heaven

& says   yes now
they're chasing
everybody

ANSELM HOLLO

THE EMPRESS HOTEL POEMS

1

just get up
and sit down again. then
    you can watch the dust
      settle.
or wait for the Irishman to come round
knock on your door again. twice
    he's asked me
first, the time, and then
"would you know of anyplehs I could get a job sirr —
      lehborin', that is."
they won't take him, he looks too
purgatorial. poor soul
8 days over from Eire
    where they have strikes.

2

the typewriter banging
better than radio   for company.
sheets of translation pile up. too many
    words, too many
other men's words
      bang thru my head. why don't they learn English
in Finland. why don't they learn Finnish Swedish German
    in England, Old & New.
they're just being kind to you, Anselm.
    they don't learn,
      you earn.

3

the old housekeeper lady downstairs
    likes the stamps. she says could you

let me have them if you're going to throw them away
        anyway. Mr Burroughs she says
     always did that, he always
         gave me the stamps. he got a lot of
            mail, too.
I give them to her. we are
      Burroughs Hollo Saarikoski Ball
        we are Mrs Hardy's
     nice writing gentlemen.

4

white smoke from Battersea Power Station
    rises   moon star London city light
beam from the airport
sweeps the sky. I switch the room light
      on and off and on, light dark light dark.
        it occurs to me
     I'm trying to tell you
        what goes on inside me.
          out there
        they'll suspect
          a Chinese spy.
ha. Battersea Beast on its back
pushing vapor puffs thru the soles of its feet
         for fun.

5

go thru my things
     god knows what you'll find. when I'm not here.
I'm not here, in this poem
I'm in another room, writing praises
        of their loveliness and terror
the long-haired beings that dance thru my mind
        not endlessly, but to be one, at one

<pre>
                    with them
                I want to be.
            I want to be one,
        I want her to be one
      when the voice begins
    she is, and she dances.
I am the voice. I praise.
there is
no mind.
</pre>

6

to return and find
2 men in grey suits who have come to look at me thru their eyes
    and say Mr H. is this yours? you know they're illegal
        in this country. oh I didn't know.
    well they are, you better get rid of it. ok.
they go, and I think
    it is a good thing to have more than one room.
what would they say
if they found what I have
in the other poem.

ELEGY

the laundry-basket is still there
though badly chewed up by the cat
but time has devoured the cat
entirely

THROUGH TWO LAYERS OF GLASS

through two layers of glass
the far end of this restaurant
a man
whose head is
a glob
of light
like anybody's
any body
he is formless form
by means of maya
& all her daughters, assumes
innumerable forms
of which i am one, eating out alone

THE DISCOVERY OF LSD A TRUE STORY

the dose of a mere
fifty micrograms totally altered
the consciousness of professor albert hofmann
motel   soda   works   intersection
swerve   hit   geode   albert
inadvertently
inhaled it
blast   core   city   ominous   rock
spiraling   rites   of   light
inhaled his   consciousness
& exhaled
"phew!   wow!   pow!   *zat* voss somsink!"

41

STRANGE ENCOUNTER

megalomaniac
midgets
exist
but
uneasily.
yes,
officer.
no,
officer.
my name is
kid sky.
i live in
the elevator.
"you're under arrest."

SCRIPTURAL 1
for Ted and Alice

boys play.
mind is.
horses travel.
thought roams.
man sees.
money paves.
farmers plough.
birds fly.
i pursued my walk.
night came.
she came to receive their form.
it was flat on top.
his head was covered with a
   brown wig, faded & shrunk from

time & use, a fringe of thin
grizzled hair showing below it
at the sides, & corresponding to
his ragged whiskers. his ears
were huge. his eyes were large.
they were green. they were

i shall only add that when i
awoke i was sorry because i
found that my golden
scales had vanished.

LOS SEDENTARIOS

most of the time we sit down
to write 'sitting down' down

Mark Twain made a contraption
enabled him to be funny in bed in writing

Goethe and Hemingway
risked varicose veins at the highdesk

sitting down we get
fat round the ass

short poems
not too frequent
are the least fattening

if you're sitting down while reading this
now is the time to get up

GOOD STUFF COOKIES

2 gods
2/3 cup hidden psychic reality
2 teasp. real world
3/4 cup sleep
2 cups sifted all-purpose iridescence
2 teasp. good stuff
1/2 teasp. pomp & pleasure

beat gods   hidden psychic reality
real world and sleep together
sift together iridescence   good stuff
pomp & pleasure
add to real world mixture
drop by teaspoon
2 inches apart   on cookie sheet
press cookies flat
with bottom of glass   dipped in sleep
bake at 400 F   8 to 10 minutes

2 dozen cookies   good stuff

Cinda Kornblum

photo by Morty Sklar

I come from Newton, Iowa (or more precisely, Wittemberg—a thriving town in the 1800's before the railroad went through Newton); attended the last of the country schools where I sat at a desk my father had carved his initials in; attended college with a Maytag Scholarship — first the U. of Northern Iowa, then the U. of Iowa where I got a B S in Sociology in 1972 (the statements in "Late Night At Hamburg Inn" mostly unproven theories from a seminar on daydreams); married to Allan, The Toothpaste Press & the garden in West Branch; currently working as Account Clerk at the University Hospitals in Iowa City & editing the *Actual Now & Then* newsletter. Another one of my poems, "In Iowa" has just appeared in the PUSHCART PRIZE II: BEST OF THE SMALL PRESSES.

Influences: Iowa rhythms, hot summer nights, Alfred Kreymborg; a way of wondering about everything, from Steve Toth & Josephine Clare; and the encouragement & support of all the Actualists, especially Allan & Dave & John.

Some of these poems have appeared in the magazines *Gum; Me Too; New York Times; The Spirit That Moves Us*, and the following book.

Book:

BANDWAGON, The Toothpaste Press, Box 546, West Branch, Iowa 52358; 1976

HEY ANIMAL – EAT THIS POPCORN

If you want to lead a calf
you have to know everything about yourself –
A full skirt flapping in the wind may threaten him
Every movement calculated, slow
as though you are a part of the earth
growing imperceptably
toward the animal

It is my hand that is feeding you daily
It is my hand you can trust

Then WHAMMO!
You and the calf are at the fair
You have taught him to trust you
so he won't jump at the applause
won't kick the kids who offer him popcorn
so he'll stand tall & square
when the bidding begins

SUNDAY

Yesterday I went to pick up the sack

of groceries

    & hit myself in the jaw.

Today I dropped the whole salt shaker

in the applesauce.

If that's love then I feel it strongly.

EVERY DAY I GO TO WORK

1

Every day I go to work.
I order rabbit anti-mouse serum
and liquid paper.
When they come in I check them off.
Then I go home.

2

Every day I go to work.
While I am taking my break
the girl relieving me comes in.
"May I speak with you in the hall?" she says.
When I get there she explains:
"A patient came in & I stamped his papers
TEAM III then I noticed on his card
that he's TEAM I. What should I do?"
I tell her to write a I over the III.
She thanks me very much.

3

Every day I go to work.
Some days, when the girls think my shoes are dirty,
they look at their shoes and say
"Remind me to polish my shoes."

OIL SPOTS IN EVERY PARKING PLACE

Oil spots in every parking place & Aha! I think
everyone who shops at the A&P

has a leaky car like mine & I spy
a piece of paper stuck to the place next to mine.
It is a dollar bill! — no a list:

> Lentils
> Beans (2 kinds maybe black & pinto or whatever)
> 4 pkg. Riceland Rice (brown)
> Tuna (cheap but not flake)
> Beef or pork liver
> Broccoli (unless wilted)
> Lean hamburger or ground chuck

I add catfood & eggs and go on in.

SEQUITOR: A LOVE POEM
for Allan

After ice-ages   comes heaven & hell
After oceans   come plains & plants
After Eisenhower   comes you, my dear

After "old man"   comes the undertaker
After temptation   comes "overdrawn"
After forgetfulness   comes the foam

After illusion   comes sadness
After profit   comes the ordinary
After employability   comes the mobile home.

A FLOWERPOT IS AN ASHTRAY

A flowerpot	is an ashtray.
A can of beer	is an ashtray.
A shoe	is an ashtray.
A litterbox	is an ashtray.
A toilet	is an ashtray.
A shirt pocket	is an ashtray.
The sidewalk	is an ashtray.
An aspirin box	is an ashtray.
Mashed potatoes	are an ashtray.
A bed is	not an ashtray.

THE HONEYMOONERS

When a youngster
I thought they were saying "celery"
not salary.
The green crisp stuff
somehow a focus of the grown-up world.
My father didn't have a
salary: he had a farm.
And just as I wondered what city folks
did with their garbage if they had no pigs
I wondered why wives nagged their husbands
to ask the boss for more celery.

College years solved the celery question.
Along with the mayonnaise & ketchup
celery was the only food still in the refrigerator
at the end of the month.

WHILE THE GARDEN GROWS
(for Allan)

Morty calls from a halfway house
either he's got car trouble
or a new girl. Our friends are so
predictable and we are too.
You have tried to draw a picture
of society's pliers —
I have tried to write a poem about Mason jars
We had to try it to know it wouldn't work
How else would we be here together now listening
to the rain while the garden outside (hopefully) grows.

ABC'S

Dog goes after Cat
Cat goes after Bird
Bird goes after Air

LATE NIGHT AT THE HAMBURG INN

*"A little bit of choice makes a color regular. A little big
of black makes dinner necessary."* —Gertrude Stein

A new blue notebook can make anyone a poet,
but an old dusty Greyhound
whisking someone into the black of night
sends one immediately to the Hamburg Inn
where I sit now

watching the door expectantly.

There were once those who knew the sun
knew the stars, knew all the answers.
If only one of them would walk in
I would recognize him instantly
and could invite him over
for tea or mead or coffee or saki. . .
Oh, the many futures that come to mind.
Time to watch them all at the Hamburg Inn.

    Setting: alone at the Hamburg Inn
    Time of day: early evening
    Who's involved: a young man, smiling, dark eyes

    Description: He walks in, sits down & we converse easily &
      intimately.   I begin:

    "I have always had a strange fascination
    with vacuum cleaners
    and monsters that look like vacuum cleaners
    and women who ride vacuum cleaners
    across the plush white carpet
    cleaning ashes
    from their loved ones' pipes."

    "My fantasies have many alternate endings"
    he says, adding salt to his tenderloin, then continues,
    "I have dreamed of giving bras to the wind &
      —watching the wind parade through town proudly
        encased or
      —of the wind violently ripping the bra from its breast
        to run naked again through the trees or
      —of the wind growing old and sagging until the bra no
        longer supports the breast

> *but drops*
> *to its knees*
> *to catch it*
> *lovingly."*

But someone has burst through the Hamburg Inn door screaming,
"Is the grill fired up? Is the grill fired up?
I wanna know is the grill fired up?"
"That guy's really drunk" I say routinely to the next table & revert
back to my silence.

In my daydreams,
I pose questions to myself
and answer them in many possible ways
rehearsing the lines knowing that
when the situation comes up in reality
I do not know what I'll say
till I hear my voice speak the words.
If only I knew what state I'd be in
or who I'd be with or how old. . .
Plans can be made but the time
can only be right
when we've almost forgotten about it

I look at the clock.
The restaurant echos with the sounds of
now-retired cooks cursing
over the hot grill
as one table rates the food
and another table rates a movie.

Suddenly my friend is back & we burst into rhyme-verging-on-song:

> *Rated R for revolting*
> *Rated P for patronizing*
> *Rated X for extra dollar to get in*

Rated R for racy dialogue
Rated P for practically boring
Rated G for god damn kids make too much noise

Rated S for sappy sentiments
Rated N for normal sex scenes
Rated B for blood & guts in living color...

The other customers gladly pick up the song & we sit back
knowing that the waitress will soon fill our coffee cups
and ask for a nickel apiece.

The sun is hot.
The sun is really hot
but it's not just the heat, it's vinyl heat!
The heat of the vinyl reminding me that nothing is real,
as the waitress makes me say I want cream
before she gives it to me
AND IT'S NOT EVEN CREAM!
I WANT MY MONEY BACK
YOU SAID THIS WAS CREAM
I scream it at the top of my lungs
and the plaster on the ceiling starts to crumble.
The cracks form letters, then words —
It is a message!
I am suddenly a member of this odd group at Hamburg Inn.
"You are the chosen ones" the plaster says
and I wake up instantly
THIS IS NOT ONE OF THE FUTURES POSSIBLE

Many times I've sat here
with the clock looking at me
surprised as I am now
pulling on my coat
debating (or not debating)
about a tip for the waitress

the waitress who I will remember
not as an employee
but as the restaurant itself.
Just as the waitress is employed
so am I & it is time to go.
It is time to go and I cannot go yet. This is the time when
everything comes back to me I had so much to say and I wanted
the evening to continue I am on my feet now and near the door
and I don't want to go so I linger forever

Morty Sklar

photo by Marcia Plumb

Born 1935 in Sunnyside in the Borough of Queens, N.Y.C. My father Jack was a Russian Jew who in 1907 at age 10 sailed past the Statue of Liberty into N.Y. Harbor. I'm fortunate to have had him so long— until last week. My mother Selma's parents were Polish and Austrian. I'm grateful for still having her.

I'm finishing a first novel, GETTING UP. Began writing at age 6 with letters home from summer camp. Slid thru Newtown High in Corona, Queens. Flunked out of N.Y.U. College of Engineering. Volunteered for the draft in '54. Jumped out of planes. Courtsmartialed 4 times, for a.w.o.l., disrespect, disobedience, etc. My 14 months in the disciplinary barracks was the best time, til then, of my life. I was relieved of having to decide what to do. I played chess, learned to type, wrote philosophical sayings in a notebook, won a weight-lifting contest.

Dishonorably discharged in '56. Went to Queens College at night and worked for my father in his small hardware store. Took a fiction course with Dr. Glicksberg at The New School. My stories came back marked "too much generalization", "show what you're feeling — don't *talk* about it".

Moved to Manhattan in 1960 at age 24, to my own apartment, with alto saxophone and typewriter. Worked as a lunch counterman for Whelan Drug chain; met my first adult friends at the Greenwich Village store. Got into dope: from grass & drugstore speed to heroin and 5 years of being strung out, in and out of hospitals, jail, the nut house...

In 1966 ran into Victor Biondo, an ex-junkie hired by N.Y.C.'s Mayor Lindsay, and helped start Phoenix House, a therapeutic community for addicts. Graduated from there 2½ years later. My first true love went back to Denver in '70. The novel didn't work. Poems. Poems came like breath. Chief initial influences: Kerouac (his prose), a friend Harris Drake, musicians Charlie Parker, Thelonious Monk, Charlie Mingus, Bud Powell, poetry workshop with Isabella Gardner — 12 *different* kinds of poets; later — Frank O'Hara.

In July '71 I scooted off in my red Honda "Dream", for the National Poetry Festival. Audrey Teeter said "Iowa City is a nice place to live", so I tried it. Thrived in the open, expressive and individualistic community of poets who had made their homes here. Was turned down twice by the Writers Workshop after BA/English, '73.

In '75 my friend Jim said "Why don't you do a magazine?" I liked the idea — a way to get into the guts of the literature world, and to "define" my own aesthetic.

Been in love a few times; been involved many times. I agree with King David, Jesus, Woody Allen, my mother, Billie Holiday and the Beatles — Love is where it's at.

Most of these poems have appeared in or are accepted for *Me Too; Midatlantic Review; Alive & Kicking!; Abraxas; Free Flowing; Dental Floss; Phoenix House News; The New Pioneer; The Spirit That Moves Us*, and the following books.

Books:

RIVERSIDE, The Spirit That Moves Us Press, P.O. Box 1585, Iowa City, Iowa 52240; 1974

THE FIRST POEM, Snapper Press (available thru The Spirit That Moves Us Press, above); 1977

THE NIGHT WE STOOD UP FOR OUR RIGHTS: Poems 1969-1975, The Toothpaste Press, Box 546, West Branch, Iowa 52358; 1977

JARASHOW

Ancient store of olden time
on Jamaica Avenue . . .

Old woman
    in black shawl
        zinc grey hair
    & grey face:
            "I remember you, you were six
            when you came around
            with your father."

(Yes, Mrs. J
    I don't remember you
  but I've been here
        somewhere

    The dust which
      should be dirt and filth
        isn't, in your place
                    it's piled
            upon layer after year,
                and inventories
            nor windy doors disturb or mingle.

Handtruck up-
on which I throw cartons
of tools
    for that black and dusty place
        highceilinged of pressed tin

            steel drawers
    a hundred sizes   thousands of nuts bolts & screws
                pipes fittings & nails . . .

On 160th & 91st Avenue
a block from the old Jamaica El,
    unloading a '70 Chevy
    to a worn handtruck,
    motions are fast
    like my father's
    but not because the cartons are future,
    pieces of my life. yet
    they feel that way,
    his blood is in them.

Driving back
    thru Union Turnpike towns past Utopia
        Pk'way homes, I speak to Dad
    in my head: Mrs. Jarashow remembers me;
    I told her you mean my brother she said
        "no, you were six
        when you came around with your father. . ."
    I feel he'll be pleased
    because what's happened since
    is over
                there's time
                to finish the circle,
                talk with my father
                who began it heading a fatherless
                brood,
                        rushing
                            til now.

I being wellfed
            had gone another way
        blessd it comes to this
        as in old times
        when sons came home.
    Once, Home was a direction Thatway,

now it's where I am, my father's house
is one place.

When Jarashow's was new
with maple counters and zinc boxes,
when a young man with his woman
stood in the doorway

my father was selling hardware & tools
from joblots, boxes and Grandpa's cellar . . .
at 35 he'd made mistakes,
was starting out again,
he

who hustled in the streets
of Jersey City, downtown Manhattan,
Astoria
my father who (he never let on til *I*
did it) took chances,
made a bundle in woolens on daring,
lost, bought a barrel of peanuts
and peddled them
from a furnished room.

Father, see,
I too have aimed
for what I want
— a little late and unsure,
but now it's the same.
I won't wait
for graveside poems —
there's time before Kaddish
and everything's okay
between you and me.

1970

POEM WITHOUT THE WORD LOVE

(1) In Rousseau's jungle
    where knifed tiger
    chews a man,
    what's to be learned?
    I've forgotten,
    but that seems to be its own reward.

(2) What I enjoy most
    has been made rubbish of:
    sneakers, transistor radio
    and salami & cheese.
    Now when I think sandwich
    I feel responsible.

(3) With each postponement
    of going for a sandwich
    I'm given a poem.
    Usually with just the promise
    of that
    I've gotten what I want.

(4) I'm sitting out here
    without a sandwich.
    Moral decisions are made alone...
    but together
    we're happy.

CHARLIE PARKER

Exploiting the medium

for all it's got

    Bird flying forever

wait a minute
I'll get my saxophone

    Lady Be Good
    in four-four
    play a warped piano til it straightens out

I'm not always lonely
are you?

    bablee *doo* dah
    bablee *doo* dah

I PUT THE TELEPHONE BACK ON ITS RECEIVER

The coleus bloomed
the lamp spoke to a book
my watch basked in the light
a load of air poured thru the transom
the wandering jew climbed out of the pot
the blanket gathered and almost got out of bed
the inverted mop spoke to something in the wall
posters and reminders hung by their fingers out of breath

and the refrigerator started up,
while the soft motor in my chest went thump
for the one billion four hundred fortyfour million
eightysix thousandth time.

MODERN TIMES

Oh Goofy,
tapdancing in the kitchen
in the moonlight
of streetlight
Oh dripping faucet
song of environmental unconcern
beauty of waste
we sing

Oh Coney Island
thrill of dying
25 cents by the ocean
laughing entrance to Fear
a dozen clams on the halfshell

Oh salt air, hot sauce

Oh my
Daffy Duck saltwater taffy
3 shots for a quarter
Oh sweet rag doll reward
Midnight in Flatbush
Oh closing of the eternally open steeplechase
trashy windy blacktops of the sauerkraut mustard
cotton candy night

Oh Light

Oh subway home
Oh home
Star Travellers of Brooklyn
Moonlight on the oil slick
Oh Mark Twain
of the green condom river,

Ellis Island ghosts
Liberty

Oh say
can you see

MENDING

The mending pillow is set against the wall
three hours before dawn.
There's no thread in view, no darning
needles — there's only the mending woman
propped against the mending pillow
on the low flat bed.
No shirts, no socks, nothing but a landscape
of leaves and vines stretched beneath her.

What can one bring to the mending woman
when her hands rest quietly upon her nightgown,
and the pale moons of the street
bathe her north facing garret?
Oh sure, your socks
are worn thru, and there's the shoulder
of your knit shirt, snagged on a splintered
bannister climbing the garret stairs.

She looks ahead, in the direction
of the vertically-slatted closet
beneath the sloped ceiling,
as tho she is looking at you.
Suddenly the silence gathers in your belly;
it shines in the mending woman's face.
At dawn
you relish the feel of your big toe
thru the hole in your sock.

IN MEMORY OF MY BEING LATE

A preserve jar
filled with flowers,
you're now in the poor side
turn-of-the-century Brooklyn.

There's a young woman
with long skirt,
hot potatoes in a pushcart

there's Lil from Flatbush
and an ocean of hotdogs
& trolleys, cabooses, beaus,
Original Whitman Samplers.

Over the bouquet,
over trees in the street
and chimneys, roofs and smoke
over a cloud
and tv aerials, flying saucers
maybe,
the Second Coming,
all
the way
to your house

THE SMELL OF LIFE

Rubbing alcohol
and a breeze from an open window,
warm February day.

Dust on the sill.
Rubbing alcohol and
infrared-heated beef mashed potatoes and stringbeans
much the same as rubbing alcohol
ham french fries and broccoli.

Later, on the way to the tv room, the gymnasium,
in striped cotton robe
my breath tastes like dinner
like all the dinners.

The rubbing alcohol
touches at once
tonsilectomy, Mother's hemmorhage, split
skull, strangulated hernia,
varicoscelectomy, intravenous methamphetamine,
hepatitis, electroshock,
junk.
                    Rubbing alcohol
— fearful but
inexplicably good
like gasoline and sewage
at lower west side service stations and piers
where the family car sometimes took us
to relatives across the river,
furry arm of my mother,
aftershave of my father
standing midstream
at the prow of the ferry
a breeze across our faces.

SO THIS IS EARTH

So this is Earth,
neat roads
between hills

My hand
over croppt grass
where the slope meets the shoulder,
I hook & twiddle
my middle finger

I allow the clouds to rise
and the trees to stand,
my body
yawns
til I can't tell the difference

Arms
like an armchair,
the speed of the car is slow
compared to my size,
the trees patient
as British subjects

the road a rolling
in whatever direction we head

MA

Ma
here I am.

your boy.

I have a degree now
and friends.
I'm sitting where
20 year olds begin their lives,
listening to Chicago's
"you are my love and my life,
you are my inspiration."

My elevator is ascending Ma,
it won't ever come down again.
Rising, but not above;
I look around: whatever's there
I want, whatever's there
is mine

Mom om so high
I've one foot in Harlem
the other in the sky.
Come with me
come on, sit on my shoulders and see
the world you gave me.

John Batki

photo by James Legault

Well, trying to be the Laziest Actualist takes some doing. For one thing, ya gotta be on the move, so one moves, from the Carpathians to Upstate (N.Y.) to Downstate (the City) back Upstate again, then Whammo! it's the Midwest, Iowa City, then back to N.Y. then out to California and now "back East" again, this time it's Cambridge. Out to lunch for 34 years now, vacillating from writing to painting, Watch Out! Max Jacob. Besides all that body movement, my heart and soul have skipped/flown from Rilke and Klee to Attila Jozsef and on to too many poets to name other than the most bedazzling: Robert Creeley, Philip Whalen, Ed Dorn, Wm. Burroughs, Jack Kerouac, Ted Berrigan, Anselm Hollo, Darrell Gray, Andrei Codrescu, Bob Grenier, Zoltan, Charles Frazier. Lucky to be born now, I guess, tho sometimes feel crammed full of all the personalities of the day. Actually we are all working on one vast collab.

Some of these poems have appeared in the magazines *TriQuarterly; The Spirit That Moves Us*, and the first and third books, following.

THE MAD SHOEMAKER, The Toothpaste Press; 1973 (o.p.)
ATTILA JOZSEF: POEMS & TEXTS, Carcanet Press (Europe); 1973; & University of Iowa Press, Iowa City, Iowa 52240; 1976
FALLING UPWARDS, Dolphin Editions, P.O.B. 313, Cambridge, Massachusetts 02138; 1976

SABINE

Last night in the rain I was frightened
but I clowned with you, Sabine.
You started the evening as a teenager,
youngest of the party, and by dawn you
aged 20 years, emerged as a woman
from a sea of looks and willpower.
Your scandic seaweed beauty, arching
little breasts (and oh the entire male-
female complex of emotions) played an
important part in my developing speech
acne in your direction. But you, I'll
never understand, accepted my invitation,
sighing "Yes" "Yes" in an unthinkingly
volatile and filmic manner. These thrills
proved to be deceptive. What was it
that made you play the straight man
to my clown I still don't know.
Was it the blue horse of your loneliness
shying at the thunderclaps of desperation?
Beyond those plosive "Yes's" and the sarcastic
change of personae you underwent from night
to morning (watched by both of us)
I have no clue to the motivation
behind your steadfast valor.
After breakfast at the Grand Hotel,
we walked arm in arm in the park.
I loved your black tulips then, Sabine.

TOURISTICISM

In the eye of the volute, we are

69

all the same. There, where
the palmetto cleverly masks
the intersection of echinoderm
and catharsis, lies the ancient
prodigy of dreams. Typically
pulvinar, it represents no ethnic
voice, and sounds the susurrant berry
for the famished hemlines.
"Appear in togas!" the command
was given, yet no one obeyed,
for the architecture of authority
had crumbled, it was the 3rd
century B C. By now people
came to stare at the eye, bored
of balteus and echinus, toting
Kodaks of terminalism.

DOWN THE BLOCK

Herbert, the corner philatelist, tells me
        that sales are up. The snow quietly
        lies in the air.

Molly, the downstairs pragmatist, is out
        with her dog for a walk. Her plump
        dark thighs are bare.

What should we do? The wind does not answer,
        the trees stretch their arms, the snow
        does not care.

Let's have some music! The dog turns around,
        shakes his head, and says, "Melodies
        are rare."

NIGHT AND DAY

for Frank O'Hara

Hotbeds of colors and an entire language of old
steamer trunks wrapped in lace and leather of Persia,
feather & foam of distant seas,
if I could have seen your eyes.

Walking the city streets the grease of short fries
and kitchen smells bow down on your path
of swimming pool detentes and ancient Texan parties,
breakfast eggs cooking to your taste,
spongy, cavernous corporations unafraid of your mouth.

Delight in eights and foursomes, reptilian disasters
in the park, dualism gathered by your side solitary,
unbuckled and confident that no evil is unknown
or unforgiven though unforgettable, you the three
of hearts draw a hand over your broken nose.

Day comes stealthily in Riviera sneakers
from its vacation in the Occident, your favorite
jewel thief who robs the night of its stars, careless,
in a white shirt, as you close your eyes.

MALLARME ON JULY 14, 1889

Mallarme liked his wine. Some of his favorites were Chateau
Haut-Brion, Chassagne-Montrachet, and the ever-mellow red
"Paisano". He also liked the color orange, and long walks
under the plantains on the boulevards. "Publishers, pub-
lishers", Mallarme murmured on the afternoon of July 14,

71

after a pleasant stroll in the course of which he observed
the people of Paris dancing on the streets. His fingers
leafed through the heavy dictionary lying in his lap.
He picked out a verdant bouquet of verbs, adjectives,
nouns, and other lesser parts of speech to present to
his publisher. Mallarme was wearing a dark flowery tie,
flowery not in the sense of the imprinted pattern, but
in the configuration of the tie around his neck. Perhaps
"butterfly" is a better description of the tie's lavish
folds, a fluttering of dark wings under the poet's chin.
Mallarme thought of himself in a perambulator as an infant,
the 1843 edition of Mallarme, was that the same Mallarme
as the young man who walked with a long loaf of French
bread under his arm twenty years later, or the Mallarme
now sitting in his comfortable fauteuil, reading the
evening paper? "Here, Fido!" he called to his dog, an
overweight Saint Bernard. Mallarme despised the papers;
Mercure de Paris or *Sentinel de France*, it was all yellow
journalism. He threw down the paper and picked up a copy
of the *Revue des Deux Mondes*, fresh from that day's mail.
Ah, another article by the Freres Goncourt! Biting into
a still warm croissant, Mallarme perused the sheet, pen-
sively stroking the back of his chocolate seal-point
Siamese, Cleo. The entrance of the maid disturbs his
ruminations: "M'sieur . . . the asparagus man is here. Will
there be anything today?"

LOVE POEM

I am a traveler
for life
tourist on earth
alone, in company

and now it's you
and me
in Marin County,
home of the electric guitar

THE INVENTION OF THE GUN
(Memoirs of an Assassin)

I lived next door to a big yellow knifethrower who
always laughed at me and mocked me and pushed me
around. There was a woman in the story, as usual.
I swore revenge and went out to find me a knife.
When I found one as big and sharp as the yellow
knifethrower's, I returned. In a dream I saw him
lying on a hillside and I saw myself plunging the
knife into his defenseless left side. I awoke and
went out with my knife and when the big yellow
knifethrower saw me, he laughed like a bird of prey.
I took a few swipes at him; he evaded these with
a smirk and a sidestep. Then, brandishing his knife
he started for me and I couldn't stand my ground.
I retreated before his terrible strokes; I turned
and ran, with him right behind. It was a miracle
that I escaped. Perhaps he killed me, and I only
dreamed of my escape.

Then I thought of a gun. I invented the gun, the
elephant killer. At the intersection of the
hairlines in the telescopic sight of my heavy weapon
I saw the big yellow knifethrower helpless, not
knowing what hit him, thrashing on the ground.

Darrell Gray

photo by Morty Sklar

Born in Sacramento, California, 1945. Grew up in Kansas (an obscure little town in the southeast corner called Walnut, aptly named: lots of Walnut trees, lazy streams and spillways, dirt roads and rabbits). A Euell Gibbons-type childhood, then back to California for highschool & college. Back to the Midwest (Iowa) for two years duty on the U.S.S. Prairie Schooner which houses the Famous Poets School, a singularly enigmatic vessel that always seems on the verge of "going somewhere". MFA with honorable discharge in 1969. Since then a string of odd jobs: post office worker, part-time car-wrecker, grave digger, encyclopedia salesman, highschool teacher, and Consultant for the National Prune Advisory Board.

Came west again with a lovely lady who changed my life — Pat O'Donnell. Presently living in Berkeley, California — a city whose people are outnumbered only by its dogs and bicycles. Moving into fiction, but still hanging on to poetry — my first love. Casting a line in the Ocean for my limit of soluble fish.

Some of these poems have appeared in *The North Stone Review; The Spirit That Moves Us*. Most are previously unpublished.

Books:

THE EXCUSES, Abraxas Press, 2322 Rugby Row, Madison, Wis. 53705; 1970

THE BEAUTIES OF TRAVEL, Doones Press, 226 W. 21 Street, No. 4R, New York City 10011; 1970

SOMETHING SWIMS OUT, Blue Wind Press, 820 Miramar, Berkeley, California 94704; 1972

SCATTERED BRAINS, The Toothpaste Press, P.O. Box 546, West Branch, Iowa 52358; 1974

ESSAYS AND DISSOLUTIONS, Abraxas Press (see above); 1977

THE PLAIN THAT BECAME THE MOUNTAIN, Tendon Press, P.O. Box 14098, University Station, Minneapolis, Minnesota 55414; forthcoming 1977

AN OLD SOUTHERN CRITIC TAKES A LOOK AT MY POEMS

grasshoppers, wheelchairs, rosebuds!
all those variably cloudy images

bundled up & flung at the reader as if
communication depended on an alien plug, a verbal

fire-sale, syntax slashed to the bone
& what's more we haven't the slightest

buried symbol or submerged meaning
to hold on to — total mayhem — "with this kind

of aesthetic how does he tie
his shoelaces is what I want to know"

not to mention all those dim & unemphasized
figments that flash across the page

all those parking lots preposterous similies
"the stars like tiny lawnchairs in the sky"

where did the soul go
to drag these fugitive embers from its fire

and was there a first fire, a fire fashioned
after no other, a fire of the final mind

from which we emerge like schoolboys in a dream
to bone white rivers & the fear of owls...

Say something deep, like the fear of rivers, something
pure & lean we can teach our kids

the lyric is a flexible form, I know:

birds, beasts and animals

in season sing their blunt reciprocal praises.
Mimeo machines murmur. Though that might be a

variable measure, all variance decrees
a cosmic tedium — "dialectic" we call it: nude idiom

of the thing reborn. The gentle researcher
tilts to the modular pinkness of the snow —

an erudite boy, addicted to spiral notebooks,
yoga, and the oblique "come-on" of dark girls

.... These old eyes grow older with each word,
& Ambiguity, like a pregnant queen, rules

the landscape where I sit. Ripe berries hang in tangles
over Samuel Johnson's grave — "like ornaments of indecision",

you might say.... And yet, there is an occasional
brilliant twist. I quote one poem, BAFFLING TURNS, in toto:

Asleep at 60 mph. No doubt the poet here has in mind
how much eludes him. Or, as Allen Tate succinctly said:

"For where Time rears its muted head and all appalls
We know not where we stand nor where we fall."

FOR GEORGE OPPEN

With the gaunt resolution
Of old age

Upon him, he moves —
And street-sweepers
            alike
A distinct utterance
Meant for no ear but
Overheard, succinct, allowed
As beasts are allowed
And particular slants of light
In the innermost
            gardens.
Naturally,
            that the leaves speak —
And no known form
Retract it, — a populus
Of desire upon desire, —
All centuries the same:

Sparrow's feet, —
Sea's glitter —
That the faces of men should
Lie in the small rains, should lie
And give truth
To the flesh.

SONNET FOR ALL GREEKS LIVING NOW

The Gods live in a micro-world
where they go to work without even
getting out of bed. The Gods
eat macaroni soup and dance, dance

as the universe passes under them;
they're so great. The Gods never go

78

to the bathroom, nor do they drool
a particular macaroni particle onto

their Afghans. They sit in a room
of quadriphonic stereos, as Zeus once
sat on Olympus, bickering with Hera.
They lift their wine glasses slowly,

as if to see in the sudden surface,
worlds their imaginations might bless.

THE MUSICAL APE

I dream continually of a musical ape
Who writes poems in his sleep
And wakes to find them published in
The Paris Review.
            This does not
Startle him. He is a good poet, addicted
To long walks, admiring
The delicate twists and turns
History has made in
His life.
        Night by night, the poems
Grow...He becomes famous
Simply by doing nothing, by being
Himself.

Often a giant page
Seems inserted from above —
This makes the dream glow
Almost like the sky, just before he wakes.

IN JUNE

A sundial spins beneath her eyes
As she wades through highschool into the dark
Despite complications and among the paper
Airplanes whirring around her
Up the narrow path into my heart

She's just an example of how one can love
Beauty clinging to its dress
Though dark be blown against it in its spiral pattern
Forming the pop-art flowers we can take or leave
Beneath the tenacious trees while down the path

A wild herb grows and there's a bongo player
Beating his fists against the seasonal
Downpour of leaves, tickets, buttons
And the thought of Shelley sailing his paper boat
Because some goddess blessed him, and the air

ODE TO JIBBERISH

I live in a jungle,
pull open the curtains,
and write what comes to me.

The natives are restless
in their brand new cars.
But small-pox is on the decline,
the gas stations open all night . . .

What if my world,
this world
between all others,
is jibberish,
what about it then?

Bird in the bush — you
be my audience, clap
and ignite the twig-tips,
rock the worm-fed nest!

It's to you I write
now, you more than
the natives, more
than the cellophane skirts
of the girls I love.

What a crackle
of iambs! What a shower
of broken syllables,
and so many parties
to celebrate the Thud!

The streets — jibberish,
cars but a jibberish
speeded up.
I'm glad I don't own a car.
I remain a simple man,
slightly intoxicated,
surrounded by jibberish,
and dedicated to the proposition
that all propositions
are jibberish, though some
more beautiful
than others.

The sun transforms

hydrogen into light.
The purest jibberish of all!

And in the park
where my nature bids me to wander
the trees which start from the ground
so firm and definite, end
in a lacy entanglement —
a cascading jibberish of leaves.

Bronze curling leaves clog up
the Neo-Classical fountain.
And there we have a condensed
little jet of cold water, spurting
a hazy mist, taking its time.

And lovers mumbling phrases from Proust,
with cough-drops in their mouths
and looking hungry.

Ah
there are so many kinds of jibberish —
you can take your pick.
But don't be a philosopher —
dig right in
and grab a handful!
Smell it.
Taste it.
Watch it grow wings.

Oh girls,
peanuts and foxtrots,
sonnets of clouds
in the household
of the sky!
All whirling,
all red-hot

and azure-deepened —
the morning is more than
bacon and eggs,
the evening more than
a glass of wine!

Put anything into the world and soon as you leave it
it beds down with the nearest soft object
and whispers its name.

But it's of you I sing,
sweet jibberish —
language of cows and alley-cats
and infants pulled from the womb.

A cry slices the twilight
and runs away through the trees.
Anthologies fall open to admit the poem,
but it's gone — a loon's song
drunk on the lake.

I've given up trying to
perfect my form.
Why should I let my poems out-do me
at what I can't be myself?
Keep on, diabolical and fragrant mushroom
towering above the insect world below.
It's you we aspire to.
Keep on, terrifying and sugary crocodile
of the soul!

The myths are coated.
The teeth of jaguars inhabiting
narrative poems
have gone home to bed.

And you, kind listeners —
what do you have in your mouths?
Jibberish hard as a gumball
that never dissolved.

Baudelaire was right.
Proust was right.
Cezanne was right.
Bullfrogs at home in their ponds
salute us, lethargically croaking the leisure
nature affords them.

And dogs in alleys rub their backs for relief
on great compositions.
Their howls of aesthetic appreciation
piss us off in the night.

How many tongues
do you speak,
how many feet do you walk on,
how many holes do you fill?
Kant tried to trap you
in his Categories,
but you flew, star-struck,
straight in his face!

God heated you up —
you boiled,
and he ate you for breakfast,
but still you survived.
You shot out fibers
thinner than any spider's,
and entered the finite orgasm,
making it grow.

You who always knew yourself

in the close-fitting cage of the parrot,
all my words become you
but if I give you a name
you laugh at it,
change it, whirl it
till it burns my tongue

and still in the heart the blood runs away from itself,
to meet you,
and bring you back.

THE ART OF POETRY

Write only
to young boys—they
are the best readers.
Women get wound up
in dreams, they see
in your images more
than you mean. But if
you mean more than
you say, write also
to women.

Jim Mulac

photo by Morty Sklar

"Jim Mulac was born in the suburbs of Chicago in 1943. When he was eight his family moved to a small farm in Iowa. He went to a one-room grade school and enjoyed a pastoral childhood during the early 1950's. His heroes were Roy Rogers and Ernie Kovacs. In high school he was deeply impressed by James Dean, along with William Blake, Robert Browning and Ray Charles.

Jim was a writing student at the University of Iowa, with a year away at San Francisco State College. Many things affected him in these years, especially Miles Davis, Eric Dolphy, Nathanael West, Kerouac, Ginsberg, and his college friend Dave Margoshes, a fellow writer from New Jersey who lived and breathed Faulkner and Ornette Coleman.

After college, Jim lived in Boston where he attended readings at the home of Steve Jonas. He returned to the Midwest and wrote o- bituaries for a year for the *Rock Island Argus*. In the late 60's he lived in the hills north of San Francisco, followed by 2½ years as a city reporter again in the Mississippi Valley.

Since 1972 he's lived in Iowa City, except for a two month stay in New Orleans and a year in Chicago. During most of the past five years he's been fortunate to eke out a meager living by playing solo piano. For the next two years, however, he'll be compromising part of his time to operate a used book and record shop, where the the spirit of Actualism will prevail."

These poems have appeared in the magazines *The Destruction Of Philadelphia; Me Too; Dental Floss; The Spirit That Moves Us.*

AFTERNOON AT THE MOVIES

You are the star
& I'm watching your final picture.
Barely 20, it's clear you are a genius.
I admire everything, especially
your refusal to smoke out of doors
and the buttonless clothes you wear.
The film is about your reaction to the books you've read
and begins with Irving Stone's LUST FOR LIFE
running through Ford Maddox Ford to
THE PICTORIAL HISTORY OF HOLLYWOOD STARS.
There is the scene where you are on time for the bus
but decline to take it, or to refund your ticket
that I particularly thrill to, thinking as I watch
how your family and friends completely understood you
despite your passion for untenable individuality.
Outside the theater, inspired, though aware of the ticket
blotted against my windshield, I jam popcorn into the meter
and exclaim: "Beauty is ruthless, and so predictable!"

THE CALLER

Sitting in my car,
I talk to you on the telephone.
You are excited because someone has come
to the door, and you laugh
because you are naked.
This time I can actually hear
the knocking
but am unable to tell
who it is.

ELEGY FOR DUKE ELLINGTON

"The more you know, the more there is;
the more music you get into, the more you want."
                    --Duke Ellington

Like sweet brother Johnny Hodges dying alone
in a bathroom during the band's intermission,
the Duke became as cool as he ever wanted to be.
In the spring of 1973 I saw him in Iowa City:
74 years old, the loud snapping crack
of his finger & thumb, he was an old
man lanky as an iron tree, discreet when
he socked the machine of his hips, once
elegant and now with long, wavey grey hair
—loose and casual on his extended vacation.
Duke Ellington made a career of freedom,
"getting paid to do what you love to do."
More articulate than leaders of his world, he
could look at the keyboard & see again how easy
it would be to make a sound so beautiful anybody
everywhere would know how madly he loved us.

WAR POEM

During the raids
the lost plane
reported
The War Over

the pilot missing.

CARS

I've watched cars acting like gods
since my baptism in gravel, when I almost
shouted that their names weren't broken glass.
But even when Steve died I said nothing.
And if his wife had lived, I might not have
said: "Watch for reflections
along storefront windows."

Somewhere alone I muttered "Christ"
the way I did Friday when Jerry Lee's car
stopped electrical power for twenty minutes.
Because I don't want to keep my mouth shut.
Not since the night those people climbed
up on the bumpers of a car
and bounced again and again.

FEELING YOU AGAIN

In a windowless room you hold a door open
showing us the snow falling, a street lamp,
old cars in a parking lot.
Soon it'll be midnight in the midwest.
I've been drinking here tonight watching
your shoulders, & thinking:
have three years touched all of you?
Quiet in your loins, like a principle,
I wait for your hand to throw a cigarette
out to the wind. I listen for the jukebox.

JIM MULAC

THE COFFEE DEN, CEDAR RAPIDS

In the window all the businessmen are
silver-haired, not wanting to look at the tall,
tattooed man at the cash register.
It is he then who picks up the change.

The waitresses between the wall & the
counter pass each other without looking.
They have amazing country voices,
too far gone for singing on the radio,
& their teeth and
sharp breasts on tv
would be too American for the world at large.
They are perfect for pie.

& I see the pie is gone,
though the lemon cream shines on
beneath the fork and the wadded napkin.
Putting this away beneath
the counter, she leans over to say:
"How are you?"
        "I'm okay."

GIRL CLINGS TO COMA

Elaine has been in a coma
for the past 25 years
the longest known
and listed in
the human unconsciousness

of world records.
She has set a human tragedy.

"At first the doctors told us
Elaine wouldn't speak to me."
Mrs. Esposito
adjusted
her dark-eyed, dark-haired
coverlet.
"But she never did."
She receives from her mother a nasal tube.

The Espositos have been told
over and over
that there is no normal. "But,
I always hoped they were wrong."

In a pink-topped hospital
kept with blue bows
she is as immaculate
as a miracle.

(1966)

THING TO WORK FOR

Today, spading out thistles,
I remember Joanna Burden's name,
and how steady and quiet Joe Christmas
worked, walking home in thick legs.
Again they teach me how to breathe, while
a thousand times, turning in the pasture,
I brush your hair from behind my eyes,

till none is left to think about.
There are the blue flowered curtains
sunbleached in the Cinora Cafe, the face
of a farmer who "won't do that kind of work",
a barefoot, fat woman in jeans, and yellow
tulips, plastic tulips in brown beer bottles
dustless to make each table nice.

SATURDAY NIGHT OUT

The entertainers are friendly
& there are more old songs now.
"The new ones don't have words yet",
they tell us, "but the tunes
are from all over the place." Yes,
these two girls are crazy, & they can
sit with us, & later we can leave,
go to another place, visit with Scott Wright
about jobs we've quit, about D.H. Lawrence
getting Scott to write again.
　　　We switch
from coffee back to beer.
The lights come on.
We go home, where the drawing still looks good.
Sunday morning, Cinda's parents call & offer
an electric broom. Spring cleaning is beginning
in February, & the abstract works that were jokes
to begin with seem more & more naturally
part of the way things get straightened out.

David Hilton

photo by Casey Stengel

Born in Albany (Calif.) Hospital in 1938. Grew up in proto-surburbia of San Lorenzo (fun in the sun). Spent banal and depraved youth hanging around jukebox, pinballs, pooltables in an underground ten-lane bowling alley; was a "pin-boy" by trade, setting several million pins and blowing teenage fortune on beer and white port. The Village Bowl is now literally buried, fit metaphor for Those Days.

Went to college between factory jobs and Army. Ended up with "ABD" from Wisconsin (Amer Lit) and landed the last teaching job in America in 1971, at a nice place called Anne Arundel Community College (specializing in the Topic Sentence) near Baltimore. Where I remain.

In 1965 or '66 met Darrell Gray in Hayward — suddenly the past 10 years of poetry lit up the sky. Through all-nights of beer and Stones, discovered everyone from Bly to Wright to Merwin, Snyder to Creeley to Ginsberg, Neruda, Vallejo — first intuitions of Actualism. Later, O'Hara and his "school" became essential to me, though only after I'd offered proper resistance. All these great poets almost at once — "Take All You Want, But Eat All You Take" — to go with an enduring love of Whitman and Roethke. . .blew my mind!

Impossible to "trace" anything — but I remember one great night when Darrell read to me *complete* the "Asphodel" poem by Williams, a poet whom I had never been "taught", who was then really unknown to me (appalling ignorance!). Since then, I've written like a hundred different poets (*very* susceptible to "influence"), but as I turn 40 the example of Dr. Williams grows ever more lucid and thrilling.

These poems have appeared in the magazines *New: American & Canadian Poetry; The Iowa Review; Poetry Northwest; Washington Review of the Arts; The Spirit That Moves Us*, and the first five following books.

Books:

THE SHOT GOES IN, Quixote Press; 1969 (o.p.)

MOVING DAY, Abraxas Press; 1969 (o.p.)

THE MAN UPSTAIRS, Modine Gunch Press; 1971 (o.p.)

HULADANCE, The Crossing Press, Trumansburg, N.Y. 14886; 1976

THE CANDLEFLAME, The Toothpaste Press, P.O. Box 546, West Branch, Iowa 52358; 1976

QUICKLY AGING HERE (anthology), ed. Geof Hewett, Doubleday-Anchor; 1969

INSPECTOR DUVAL'S TOUGHEST CASE (with Tim Hildebrand), New Erections Press; 1970 (o.p.)

RETURN TO THE RAT PLANET (with Warren Woessner), Abraxas Press; 1972 (o.p.)

MRS. AND MRS. BIG MONEY (with Woessner, Hildebrand, James Stephens), Abraxas Press, 2322 Rugby Row, Madison, Wis. 53705; 1975

WISH YOU WERE HERE! (with Woessner), Abraxas Press; 1976

THE IMMIGRANT

Today, a bush is a bush to me
and a bird, a bird. They sit
in one-word rooms in my head.

Ashore, great garden genitals
rise and flow above the walls
of the serene empress's vast domain:

in broken Poetry the best I do
is point and mumble, "Flowers?"
I own precious few sounds for *life*.

Rootlets surviving stone, plunge of green-
tipped wings into lightning dusk,
moss-softened boulders strewn down

white talus — all are foreign photographs,
but of my promised land! Well, I'm fresh
off the boat, staring hard, clutching

my ragged satchel of sounds.
I figure I'll be cheated blind.
But that's all right — I'm here.

I TRY TO TURN IN MY JOCK

Going up for the jump-shot,
Giving the kid the head-fakes and all
'Til he's juked right out the door of the gym
And I'm free at the top with the ball and my touch,

Lofting the arc off my fingertips,
I feel my left calf turn to stone
And my ankle warp inward to form when I land
A neat right angle with my leg,
And I'm on the floor,
A pile of sweat and sick muscles,
Saying,
Hilton,
You're 29, getting fat,
Can't drive to your right anymore,
You can think of better things to do
On Saturday afternoons than be a chump
For a bunch of sophomore third-stringers —
Join the Y, steam and martinis and muscletone,
But, shit,
The shot goes in.

THE MAN UPSTAIRS

Against a yellow accordian
he loses the War always. His gray voice
sings each night the kamikaze
pasting his buddy to the bulkhead.

1944. He hides the year inside
his trousers like a treasure still
alarming him. It sirens him down
the stairway that stops at my door.

He says he knows the arms of the police
are really rubber hoses
and if you give a woman an inch
she'll cut it off. And since

the silent mailman commits
only the big-time thefts (the letter
from his mother announcing her rebirth)
he knows I've stolen his dish towels

on order six years from Procter & Gamble
in Kansas City. He holds nothing personal
against Kansas City — all his friends
have vanished everywhere,

the caves go under everywhere.
And all of them were cowards anyway,
flattening themselves into extra coats
of mole-colored paint stuck

to the turrets of their battle stations
as the zeroes fell drunkenly
upon the decks. At age 18
to survive as a coat of mole-colored paint,

after the attack to be chipped off
slowly, daily by the rubber hoses of
cops, bartenders, mailmen, landlords —
is only what a coward deserves though it is hard.

For such philosophy the Government
thinks he is 100 percent and
rewards him accordingly. So he
has time for his music

that rises each night like the whine
of an ancient propeller,
keeps rising
until he throws his body against the floor.

APRIL 29, 1975

We are
at peace. It is
as if the War

were a hideously deformed
idiot child
who, despite our

best care,
finally died.
And now we grieve

over this shallow
grave
called Peace.

LATE NOVEMBER, MADISON

Across the lake the lights
of the rich people
signal a code *warm money*.
We stand in a room
where a dog is yawning, and a boy
is reading his poems
written, he murmurs, from the bottom
of a pit of acute paranoia.

A mile of late November
to those stars across the pit
of water. Farm income will fall

again this year. Massive layoffs
from the second biggest
payroll in town. And
the poetry is poor,
is terrible, and we applaud.

CELL TRANSPLANTS

Bloated, gray-mustachioed crone,
work boots broken over mutating sweatsocks,
head swathed in a black penitential shawl . . .

a bright July busstop to San Francisco,
beautiful bare-legged kids sharing french fries,
an aloof matron wreathed in weasels . . .

suddenly is shouting to me she's going to get
"Cell Transplants!"

"Cell?" I ask.   "CELL!" she screeches,

"CELL TRANSPLANTS! —
So's I can quit smoking these rotten cigarets.
Just a month of Cell Transplants,
my lungs'll be clean as a baby."

She's smiling, unwinding her shawl,
not quite toothless, not quite bald,
not quite unbeautiful.

THE SECOND PART

When the old bitch barks at the bottom of my iron backstairs
a music brims the dark flowing back home
and I'm helpless thinking *She's come!* . . .
then the noise drains and leaves
a lapping at my kitchen window. . .
tiny tongues laving a stiff lover! . . .
sometimes I even look,
she is never there.

I am trying to say that in the silence
of this city I dread
that dog's bark. . .

among the rotting garbage cans
that dumb old girl tethered on a ten-foot rope
waking in rain to howl her gray dreams. . .
what loneliness crazier than hers?
Drunken growls and whimpers rise
from her owners downstairs.

2

I confessed a year ago, "I've nothing for your birthday."
"Just write a poem for me," she said.
And I did
and (better than America!) it was
fleshed with pride and wonder
that we did love each other. . .

oh the laughter
in that poem awoke
my terror
that is its mate. . .

things have ways of evening out.

And this poem I'm willing now
is but the second part
graceless as a grieving hound
to that poem, that paean, that mock
I was so dumb to think
would need no further work.

CHRISTMAS POEM

There is nothing to complain of now
but happiness. The ice is warming itself
against the belly of a black child.
For a few hours I know that I can save no one.

Men have gathered inside footballs to warm themselves.
They are driving to the tropics in powerful ashtrays.
They are locked in a deserted drugstore, each singing
carols to his mother's beauty.

But I am taxed
only with this happiness that rose up
in the middle of the day like a golden hobo
waking to a strange
street, asking
for his son.

POEM

I want to be one of those poets
who owns a farm in Vermont or Kentucky
whose address is just his name
above the name of a town *New Charity* or *Halcyon*.

I almost cry when I think of that poet
driven from bed by the green cries of birds
and by the clean sunlight pouring in through the window
dappled and cooled by the trees right outside.

That queer *feeling* hits my belly when I think
of him cracking the crust of ice on whatever the water is kept in
and bringing the water again and again in cupped hands to his face
then drying his face with a blue flannel shirt
and putting the damp shirt on over bare muscles.

Then he walks softly into the dawn-shadowed kitchen
God! and he sits down with pencil and paper at a rough wooden
                                    table
and rubs the pencil strongly all across and down the paper
until a poem appears, which doesn't take very long.

Ah now the woman comes in, her robe does not cover her breasts
so casual and lovely as sleepily she puts the water on to boil. . .
soon the hiss of hot water poured from a pot, then coffeesmell.
The sudden barking of a hound outside silences the birds.

The poet embraces his wife in the still brightening kitchen.
He is passionately careful for she is greatly pregnant.
A breeze slips in the open backdoor and flutters the poem on
                             the rough table.
It is a poem in celebration of the coming of their child.

LAST SOUTH BALTIMORE POEM

It was not 'not wanting
to get involved' —

the wino splayed
across the sidewalk

in front of the failing
shoe repairman's, on

his back, taking the
hard, slant

October sun, his nose
a red cyst, purple lesions

beneath 4-days grizzle —
because I could shake

him and rasp *mister! hey
mister!* like a kid and

so he'd just be
dead, or I could

shake him harder
and so he'd come alive —

to what difference?
I am the man, I

*suffer'd, I was
there*. . . and got out.

Sheila Heldenbrand

photo by Morty Sklar

Born May 26, 1951 in Winterset, Iowa—the oldest of 4 children. Attended Van Meter Community School K-12, playing basketball after school. Raised on a small farm.

1969-1973, attended University of Iowa, expanding my field of reading at the university library, falling in love, writing more prolifically, and meeting other writers.

1972, married Steve Toth; living ever after in a series of "interesting" houses and doing a series of "odd" jobs.

1976, moved to LA to pursue my career in writing, supporting myself by teaching in a nursery school.

Future — hopefully bright — in script writing, poetry, art, nonfiction, and ?

Some of these poems have appeared in the magazines *Black Maria; Out There; Gum; Candy; The Spirit That Moves Us.*

Books:

MORNING GLORIES (with Steve Toth), Oyster Press; 1973 (o.p.)

THE WORLD IS GOD'S TV, The Toothpaste Press, P.O. Box 546, West Branch, Iowa 52358; 1975

PROSE POEMS, Tidewater Press; 1975 (o.p.)

GOD SAID TO THE ANGELS

God said to the angels,
should I make man?
The angels said, no,
what do you need with man
when you've got us?
so he burned them up.
Then he asked the next angels,
should I make man?
They said, sure.

THERE IS A LITTLE HOUSE

There is a little house.
Inside is an old woman.
Someone says:
The good eye projects,
the evil eye attracts light.
She has a good eye.
She has white hair.
My innermost fears
come popping out of her mouth.
She jumps onto the running board
of the red ford truck,
and whispers in the window
in my ear, "Don't worry
you're going to be happy now."

THE PRESIDENT IS NOT FUNNY

— or "How I fought the law and the law won"
— Bobby Fuller

Who in his right mind
would want to rule the world?
That's what's scarey.

There are those who want to take us over —
who say democracy is a degeneration of the feudal system.
Some bestsellers say "they've got us by our money."
Think about what you wouldn't have if they call *that* in.
And all this time they've been giving us coupons:
"Save 10¢ on your next refrigerator".

I know that feeling from when I was a thief.
SOMETHING FOR NOTHING
something happens to you.
suddenly you can have anything in the store.
you start having dreams about stealing the display windows.
you begin to think you've broken the law of the universe
and no one can stop you.

The day two plainclothes women put the finger on me
I had $1.75 past felony. In other words $21.75
or 1 — 5 years.
but they were willing to make it
3 years probation —
the same as Agnew got — because I was just a kid.

There's that tap on your shoulder
"excuse me, haven't you forgotten something?"
you and the evidence are taken away by two cops;
and you're cured of one form of materialism.

But, for Mr. International Banker,

who's to say, "excuse me,
haven't you forgotten something?"
and the cosmos doesn't have a statute of limitations.

CONCENTRATION

fly flying away
wishes it could stay,
straight haired people
in curlers,
curly haired people
with little bricks hanging
on the end of each hair.
alms for the rich —
give me what I deserve.
oh, lord,
are you the same guy i saw
yesterday?
heads, toes
tits, ass
i hear it's simple.
minds all about
delicately out of balance
like slices of pie
that don't quite come together,
like bums sleeping in a circle
their heads all pointed towards the fire
their feet all pointing towards the stars

A WOMAN NEEDED SOME MILK

A woman needed some milk from the store.
She walked to her tree and said
"John, bring home a half-gallon of milk."
That night her husband came home carrying the milk.
A man who had overheard
questioned her about this wondrous tree
and told her about the telephone.
"Oh yes, we are very poor, or we too would have a telephone."

SNOW IS FOR TRACKING THE INVISIBLE MAN

The barn was on fire.
The guards were no longer needed,
nor boots, nor cap for his head.
But people yelling out of cars
made him self-conscious anyway.
A Volkswagen topped by a red light drove by.
Red sparks like hairs on edge flew out.
First his bones appeared
then blood, nerves, finally skin, features
and a tattoo of a rose.
He built a house for himself,
a weird woman, and birds.
Why did you come back? they asked him.
For love, for love.

BECAUSE THE SAVAGE

Because the savage meets his needs with
    minimum effort,
much of his time is spent in leisure.

EARL THE PEARL

I join a group of women and children
working to break out of a large
building. They tell me they've started
a tunnel under the table. I look at it
and it is only a few inches deep. A
short guy on a white rabbit with red
eyes rides up. Some, he takes their
breaths away in baggies, some he saves
for later. Just when we think we are
going to escape, the man comes in and
asks us to deliver a bag of sugar.
Then he says, "and by the way, take
them to the ovens." We wait in the
basement for the ovens to arrive.
They are elevators. Janitors float
a few inches off the floor.
Their faces are dark and beautiful.
They just work there. It is my last sight.

George Mattingly

photo by Morty Sklar

"George Mattingly was born in 1950 in Cape Girardeau, Missouri. Little of his early life is known. His earliest recorded memory concerns watching the glare fall through a howling wind on the previous year's dead prairie grass in the early spring near his parents' house in an obscure part of southwestern Iowa. Escaping his family, he entered Phillips Exeter Academy in Exeter, N.H., 1963, and failed to graduate in 1967. He worked a year as a cowboy and swather-operator for $7/day at Marble Ranches near Deeth, Nevada, then migrated to the University of Iowa where he did not attend the Iowa Writers Workshop from 1968 – 1971. While working for a little-known advertising agency in Iowa City, he started the now-infamous *Search For Tomorrow* magazine, and Blue Wind Press, in 1970. After a brief stint as book-designer for Something Else Press in Vermont in 1973, he booked passage for a train to California where he lived the rest of his natural life as a publisher, poet, novelist and free-lance graphic designer. His career was "long and varied" to quote the inimitable prose of his major biographer, "hampered only at the end by bouts of glaucoma, ulcers and coronary thrombosis." Literary historians note ironically that what time now judges to be his greatest works (which masterfully fuse lyricism with stunning metaphysics articulated in fresh vernacular American English) were routinely dismissed in reputable literary review media of the day (publications which now seem quaintly archaic, e.g. *The New York Times Book Review, American Poetry Review,* and *Poetry*) as "sophomoric and unstudied", or "too exhiliarating to be of real worth." While biographers disagree as to George Mattingly's major literary influences (citing, among others, O'Hara, Ashbery, Parra, Oppen, Rilke and Dorn), they all agree that his works were, like those of William Carlos Williams, inherently & explicitly concerned with The World As It Is, and quite unaffected by the cumbersome artistic edifices constructed by the now-obscure prize-winning poets of his day."

Some of these poems have appeared in the magazines *The World; Chicago; Out There; Suction; Toothpaste; Search For Tomorrow; The Spirit That Moves Us,* and the middle book, following.

Books:

DARLING-BENDER (collaborations with W.S. Merwin et al), Blue Wind Press; 1971 (o.p.)

BREATHING SPACE (illustrated by the author and Tim and Karen Hildebrand), Blue Wind Press, 820 Miramar, Berkeley, Calif. 94707; 1975

SWEET DREAMS, Seamark Press, Box 2, Iowa City, Iowa 52240; forthcoming winter '77

GOD'S WORDS TO THE LAST APE

Now if you stop
& think

the world will become
a solid circuit of seasons
        lips   tears
amazement   and   space

From now on find me
in green roses
& nipples & blizzards:
                I change.

And listen, man,
        Good luck.

THE BEST THING GOING

Shutting the door
doesn't turn out the light

        Retractions say only
          "I don't know how to say it"

You scarf me up like a pilot
I keep my arms blue

        If I say I'm great
        it's because I touch you

CRUISING FOR BURGERS

The radio exploded without a sound. Then the air was filled with hundreds of little weather reports, which landed in the bushes & grass around me & crawled away.

A woman who seemed to be my friend took my hand & said "Let's go." As we walked down one smooth green hill & up another, somebody's mother swooped over us in the air, clutching a purse & car-keys.

She circled to buzz us again, but as she did, my friend put her palm on the top of my head, & the two of us flew up into the air.

Behind us, the mother fell to the grass & got old. She shook her purse at a stump, which growled. Then she turned into wood, and chunks of bark peeled off her face.

When I looked around again, I felt something hard touching my feet. The ground. The woman who had brought me here was waving goodbye from the cab of a big rig. She roared away across the muddy parkinglot, shifting gears very smoothly.

A black man took the ticket out of my hand & pointed to the train. I hoped my luggage would arrive safely.

The train climbed steadily into the mountains. Dams & rivers to the right of the tracks were overflowing. I suddenly looked around & realized I was the only passenger on the train.

The train stopped when we reached a little plateau. "Why are we stopped & why am I the only passenger?" I asked the conductor.

"Express run, mah man," he said, smiling, "but we got to wait fo da flood." He pointed out the window. Down the slope, the train disappeared into deep blue water.

I got off the train, scared some cows away from a field-stone house behind some willows, & walked in.
A calendar said "April" above a picture of a salami. My old friend Deborah Owen was draped over a green velvet sofa, jiving with some black guys in big shoes across the room.

"How long have you been in The City?" she asked, looking bored. "Just got in," I said. I sat down in a big flower pot by a computer terminal of some sort.

Donald Justice came in dressed as a nun in sandals. "Have you been helped?" he asked, pulling out an order pad.

"No, thanks," I said. He disappeared.

"Let's see yo stuff," a big black guy said to Deborah. She stuck out her tongue & pulled up her sweater.

"Your order's ready," Donald Justice yelled at me from the other room. I went to get it so I wouldn't have to stare at Deborah's beautiful little breasts.

Don showed me to my seat & turned on a movie about the life of the blue heron. The sound track was by Pink Floyd — sort of swamp sounds & electronic oozing. The heron reached into the water with his beak & pulled out a cheeseburger. He did this many times, then he flew away.

GOODBYE SONNET

Outside cool July half an hour from morning
Charlie sends love from Salt Lake / Aretha Franklin
                                              fills the room
& distant trucksounds give life a constant disguise....
Smoke occurs to the plant by the clock:
It's a thought: smoke: to the plant: are my thoughts that
real? Orange drink, for instance, results from
the planter's affection for sharkskin, a few oranges,
& lots of chemicals, with thoughts of their own.

Birds plant their wings in the sun,
Roberto Clemente goes to sleep in the sea.
I dream I am dreaming but everything's real,
the snow on TV & the pictures of you left in me,
though maybe the real you's got your thumb out by now,
in the hamburger storms that drench America
                                    with identical details.

from THE LIVES OF THE POETS

After a long evening waiting for John Wayne to blow up the
oil-well on Tim & Karen's TV, I walked toward downtown
Iowa City in the tiny echo of the last commercial for the Cap
Snaffler. I thought it was about midnite, but the bank's time
& temperature sign said it was 5:30. When I got to the Burger
Chef, there was a huge crowd out in the intersection of Wash-
ington & Clinton. Everyone was looking down toward the
theaters, shaking their heads.

I pushed my way through the crowd, heading down Washington.
Next to a huge jagged hole in the display window of Fuik's

Jewelers, Ted Berrigan and Anselm Hollo were lying on the sidewalk. Ted was halfway sitting against the wall, next to an empty gallon of Paisano, wearing twelve Bullwinkle watches on his left wrist & singing songs by the Irish Rovers. Anselm was flat on his back, looking straight up at the stars, throwing huge fistfuls of diamonds up into the air. As soon as the jewels plunked down on his wolfskin vest, he tossed them up again. A giant baggie full of Colombian Blue hung out of his pants pocket. He was saying *"Aiiieeeeeeee!"*

Anselm's lawyer, Mr. Kingsley Clarke, Jr., stood a few feet to one side, looking grim, in his non-descript but nevertheless weird suit, one hand attached firmly to his red beard. Some little birds gathered on the marquee of the theater next door, going tweet tweet & shitting on the red plastic letters that spelled out *GONE WITH THE IND.*

The grill cook from Playmore Lanes nudged me & said "It's them poets. They've got the diamonds *and* the dope."

PATIENCE, NO SPEED

Soft cheeks & all that jazz
Saturday night
out the window

Saturn's rings
weightless as the sudden thought
of your hair

Here in delerium
nerves of fur, my arms

116

                    turn brown

                  One foot

                     slips off

          coherence

                    TIDE

Branches of blood
                    in our eyes
              hold the world

                  together.

                    Wandering away,
    the warp of distance
                          involves us in time,
        the height of the new grocery store sign in the sky,

                        the postcards
    we send strangers

                        far from the depth
    of this summer afternoon

                        in the sunlight, curving &
    containing us,

                    our hands & voices

              rising

John Sjoberg

photo by Morty Sklar

Bong / i am born / everyday / currently it is / in Iowa City   Not to
say there are not those J.P. Sartre sundays
Originally i was birthed in Aurelia, Northwest Iowa town, 1944.
Barbara my Mother, Beth my Mother, Chester G. my Father & the
rolling corn plains with clumps of bouncing farmyard trees, the
Little Sioux River valley fishing walking. . .

Aurelia a town of trees & lawns; a mainstreet (one street cheers) festooned at Christmas & the end of August, the Farmers' Picnic a weekend before "school" started A vast vast mainstreet fair of vivid dimension in early childhood

. . . Really a town where rolled over the hills the earthy farmer's fields Around they did surround And we track-boys tuning up for the "Relays" wd run a "section" of blacktop / gravel / gravel / gravel / & blacktop bearing, bouncing on feet, in mind the long horizon & yellowed last-year cornstalk rows. Finally returning, dying for wind & seeing the Elevators. the grain elevators their large presences, seen at sunset, at midday in bright august, or black silhouette on the gray-white winter sky. A oneness between town & country lives there in those elevators, horizon, town.

This is why i visually held the passing towns & fields & wooded bending little rivers as i left for the City of Iowa City & the University education. I left with my '50 Chevy, blue-green with a visor.

Some of these poems have appeared in the magazines *Dental Floss; Gum; Toothpaste; The Spirit That Moves Us* , and the following book.

Book:

HAZEL, The Toothpaste Press, Box 546, West Branch, Iowa 52358; 1976

WE TRY NOT TO TOUCH SO CLOSE

We try not to touch so close to our hearts,
But the night's unavoidable mind has made us
Try to bind our lives with
Strings we cannot find.
Its deep placed calls of softness
Draw our threadful thoughts
To hearts that are not there.
This compelling conversation avoids
The definition of our indispensable sighs.
This silence is all we need. We hear
The heart of love, and wait to see
Its daylight dawning, and stay the day into eternity.

PABLO ANYTIME

you are a man, the artist gazing out at the mirror
    & back thru your arms to the canvas
                    then we, numberless years later
see you
            white blouse, orange fan of a tie!
            . . against that stroked, black background. i look
& when i look closely, see that the palette was
                        the last thing you painted.
        Orange, orange! . . is your palette
            Steady are your eyes.

JOHN SJOBERG

FANTASTIC COLLECTION OF STAMPS

I

somemore cigarettes, some buckhorn, some
   calligraphy
adis ababba touching his hat to his little

cigar, before he lights it.
   my cable from mama read "hangtight, i love you
So much!"

An albatross came in on a cycle, so you know
   we got luck. i read some of ted's poems to the
class, so we're off to a good start. infact
my cat has me completely baffled.

II

no real beginning. the beginning is now. did
you know baking soda can be used a lot. i use
ultrabright, even so; yet there are lots more ways
of using baking soda. so i don't feel left out
without something to do, when i have (baking soda).

kissed mary goodnight makes the qt. of beer taste
so good! you know i have a little pipe looks just
like a toilet stool. kind of eggnog shaded towards
a little pink. the description never gets to the
fact that i can't use it. the glaze is the kind that
makes it smooth, so smooth i can not get a screen to
stay.

III

fanny farmer "turtles" are my mother's favorite candies..
while at the same time, my favorite matchbooks are
green cross. the relevance to this evening is that
i love my mother & i like to have a cigarette now & then.

IV

the red-brown fox quickly dashed over the wheelbarrow
but remembered william carlos williams.

OVERALLS

mary wears them
light blue

she even wears a gold
sweater underneath
& no one can define how
she walks, when she is
wearing them.

o, she carries it over
when she's in other clothes,
yet have you ever seen a farmer
in a suit?

well, mary can play a flute,
either-way, but is most lovely

in her overalls.

AN ANSWER

why did george washington
try to kill himself?

it was morning and so george
had a cup of coffee. this
wasn't unusual. the ritual
of drinking a carefully poured
cup of coffee was
                        the beginning
of the day. he had red sox
on. this was a rarity for
revolutionary times. (red
dye for sox was not invented
until 1833)
                        george's cat
was playing in the bed-
room. martha had gone
for the day. she'd been
leaving the house rather
early these last few days.
she usually left with jerry,
the indian cook for the
washington family.
            (jerry was a bright young
brave, since he'd had an
education back in the early
days when he worked for the
measurement research corporation.)

                        the beginning
of the day. george looked out
of the house at the river and
all the maples that had
grown on this, his famous

plantation. george was re-
calling all the red-orange
maple leaves he'd picked
yesterday. it had been sun-
set then. their pet
peacocks had been strutting
all over the closely cropped lawn.
george felt good remembering
the peacocks. they always
reminded him of how terribly
immortal
        the washington
name would become. "ancestors
and descendents." said george
to himself in his

dove white kitchen.

THOUGHTS

You have a headache Rimbaud.
You have an ashtray on your head.
You have a headache and you're sick.
The ward has gotten your nerves
To get up to get a glass of water.
You are really tired out, tonight,
And you're awake and thirsty.

There's a pipe and tobacco
on the mahogany table.

THE DEATH OF DEMOCRACY

So, i finished another bottle of coke. while sadly
i have finished a 2nd article on the murders that
          went on in Santiago, Chile, of Allende
& his friends.

Those who committed these crimes did not come to
their Presidente's Palace like men with their guns,
or meet him face to face. Oh no! Unhuman monsters,
they stayed a very great distance away, saying, "You
have three minutes in which to surrender." Only then,
from some military base, some base hidden from all
human eyes did they send jet fighter-bombers

          to bomb the Presidential Palace.

For, all this time these monsters knew that the
people, the people of Chile, the workers gathered
together in the factories, only had handguns with
which to fight
          for Freedom won by election.

PAFFER JOCKER

        walks up to a lady
        & says, "'scuse me ma'am.
        i love green plants & i was
        just looking at yer hat an'
        i was wonderin' if you were
        a bush of some sort."

        the lady (huffed like)

grabs her latest cop & tells
the man in blue, "watch this man,
i think the cornbread is still
undone & he asked me if i had a
magnolia growing in my backyard."

BLUE TIT

Absolute, freezing, eternity,
the blue tit.
Frozen words   nothing.
An expression   nothing.
A monument   nothing.

To just wait out
the feeling I have
(to shit).

I am in
an absolute room —
no john
no place
when you have to,
no place. blue tit.

Books piled to the ceiling
Books half read
Envelopes ripped open —
one, with pink stationery
and brown ink letters
sticking out
sticking out — mouth & tongue

A cat's tongue
A canary pair of pants
Falling apart.

PORCH WINDOW

my head is green
the songs here, the bird songs
here & here & here
are my heart.

the tractor engine beats,
drives fall corn up into the granary.
my whole body can feel it. i wonder
if they'll take me into town
in a wagon.

i'll stop at your house
in a bushelbasket,
grinning from ear to ear.

Steve Toth

photo by Morty Sklar

"Steve Toth was born April 11, 1950 in Bemidji, Minnesota. He start-
ed writing very early. Just after the discovery of crayons. Grew up
in Calumet Park, Il., a Chicago south side suburb & later in Green
Acres, an unincorporated collection of humanoids. Finally gradu-
ated from West High School in Davenport, Ia. Not much is left
from all this, Toth's past being pretty much completely obscured at
any given moment by his present which is still taking place. He
was last seen living in Los Angeles' south bay region community of
Lawndale."

Some of these poems have appeared in the magazines *In The Light;
Out There; Toothpaste; Search For Tomorrow; The Spirit That
Moves Us* and the middle 4 following books.

THE GATHERING (anthology), edited by Jon Kinnamon & Rob
Robertson; 1970 (o.p.)

GOLD RUSH, The Toothpaste Press; 1972 (o.p.)

MORNING GLORIES (with Sheila Heldenbrand), Oyster Press; 1973
(o.p.)

ROTA ROOTER, Frontward Books, 334 E. 11 Street, No. 16, N.Y.C.
10003; 1977

TRAVELING LIGHT, Blue Wind Press, 820 Miramar, Berkeley, Calif.
94707; 1977

I LOVE LUCY (with Sheila Heldenbrand), In The Light, Woodridge,
Illinois 60515; forthcoming Spring 1978

THE TURQUOISE MECHANIC'S SON

i am the turquoise mechanic's son
sitting in the drive eating doughnuts.
beautiful cars — light as quick silver
my car has an agate gear shift knob
my car has a roof of broccoli
its tires strong as root beer
its interior a flour bag
blowing away in the wind

its headlights of mahogany
its dash made of water
it holds the road with loving tread
its steering wheel encompassing small talk of crickets
        and with it i hang a louie

        before me joyful
        after me joyful
        above me joyful
        below me joyful
all around me joyful
we are going for a joy ride
sound of joy when the engine turns over

ABOUT YES & NO

When the tree limb falls down
on your head,
it doesn't say yes
or no.

SYMBOLS

Things are born out of ideas.
The mind of man gets an identity from each experience,
Consequently nothing touches our attentions
Which is left unexplained to some part of us.
Where the same things are not available
They are grown in the fertile human mind.
Thus the savage has an explanation
For every experience in his world of phenomena,
And the same things shape themselves in our minds.
But just how is this accomplished?
Men and women look out
Upon anything that rises spontaneously.
What they see is far closer to depicting
What they are thinking about
Than any other symbol which they could later devise
To mean the same thing.

MAGIC SAM

perculator
perculator
perculator
perculator
perculator
perculator
perculator
humpback humpback
perculator
perculator

MORE SELF-CONSCIOUS

when i was less self-conscious
it would never have occurred to me
to look up into the face at the window
and see how much work went into that last smile.
Now i feel i must close the curtains.
Something in this room seems very familiar.
And now i see that this leg is mine to us
and with it i can walk across the room.
But now i can't remember how i got so tired.
Only that after being so tired
now i'm wide awake
but all around me
something is sound asleep.

FIGHT FIRE WITH FIRE

i eat what others throw away
i wake when they go to sleep
they think i am always asleep

nobody knows what i am or what i do

nothing taken for granted
nothing for sure

once they know you
you are never free of their thoughts

THE GOLDEN GREATS

I take to this music
like a hound takes to the chase.
My head is a lion's head.
My shoulder running out the door.
Give my regards to the weather.
Relate my laundry
to the candle,
my eyes flying into it
like moths.
Later in the Super Value
I have to leave without my change.
Pushing my cart through the streets
while people with lassos

sing about home cooking

They impress me right out of my wits.

"Be more breathless"

I tell them.
"You're supposed to sound romantic
not hungry."
And then I'm gone.

REMEMBER

two people are in the room
you and me

we look amazed they should be so life-like

132

so like ourselves
and yet so different

they move so slow
we with incredible speed

looking back
it all seems so drawn out
at least
it will never happen again

as long as there is light
to see with

all eyes are attracted to shiny things
to a mouse with infra-red eyes
our trailer is the brightest star in the night

POEM TO A POTTED PLANT

You think you have always lived
In this city,
But look
There is an ocean behind it.
The rest of you is a lamp
Made of driftwood;
But this lamp uses electricity,
And you want a lamp
That will shine because it likes you.

THE HANGED MAN

he boards the plane
but parachutes out
just after take-off

saying how could I think
of going anywhere
when I'm already here

the plane's shadow passes
as he falls & leans back
against the will of the wind

tumbling to up side down
now falling up
being in the sky comes easy

you know sometimes I think
I'm at the end of my rope
but really I'm just hanging around

MARK

x marks the spot
where the world is
filled in
now turn the page
& start in on the next

Dave Morice

photo by Morty Sklar

Born 9-10-46 St. Louis. Learned to read during car-rides with my parents. They would ask me what the electric signs and lighted billboards downtown said: Coca-Cola, Used Cars, Starlight Theater, etc. Giant colorful alphabets flashed in my eyes.

Wrote poems as soon as I could. At 5, rhyming fables about Joe the Giraffe, including drawings.

In high school, I began writing and illustrating an epic children's poem, "The Idiot And The Oddity" — 115 pages of rhyming couplets about a leprechaun named Scratch O'Flattery. Finished it 10 minutes before my 21st birthday. Then I was ready to write adult poems.

College at St. Louis University, English BA. Then 1969 took me to Iowa City for Writers Workshop. Poetry MFA, 1972.

Suddenly Actualism rose up from the Iowa City streets and scattered dust toward the Workshop. I edited *Gum* magazine to find out what was written in that dust.

Wonderful wordy love affair with Joyce Holland, Concrete poet and editor of *Matchbook* magazine. She taught me everything she knew about writing from A-Z. Without her, the blank page would be a little more blank.

Since 1973 I've done several public writing events: Poetry Marathon Number 1, 1002 poems in 12 hours; Mile-Long Poetry Marathon; Poem on Joyce Holland's dress on NBC's Tomorrow Show; Poem across a suspension bridge connecting New Jersey and Pennsylvania; Poem whitewashed in huge letters on an Iowa City street; and more.

Wrote a number of these in costume as Dr. Alphabet.

Over the past three years I've taught poetry-writing to various groups: People over 60, grade-school children, speech-and-hearing-impaired children, physically handicapped children, and mentally retarded children and adults. They've taught me a great deal about poetry and the magic markers surrounding it.

I hope to write poems publicly in all 50 states before my last word orbits the page of this planet.

Some of these poems have appeared in the magazines *Suction; New York Times; Search For Tomorrow; The Spirit That Moves Us.*

Books:

POEMS, privately published by Al Buck; 1971 (o.p.)

TILT, The Toothpaste Press, Box 546, West Branch, Iowa 52358; 1971

PAPER COMET, The Happy Press, Box 585, Iowa City, Iowa 52240; 1974

SNAPSHOTS FROM EUROPE, The Toothpaste Press; 1974

POETRY CITY, U.S.A., The Happy Press; 1977

MY BROTHER

my brother was killed
in the last war
taking a beach-head.
he wore a dress uniform
and held his hat
in the photos my mother has.
he was thin,
needed some food, she says,
holding his human face
in her shadow.

IN THE WATER

Our faces
looked up at us
from the water
with green smiles waving
to the sun.

A log bobbed
on the surface,
in yellow waves,
a sundial.

The face
in your waves
was yours —
mine was too close
to recall.

IN THE MIDDLE OF A WIND TUNNEL

And here we are in the middle of a wind tunnel
    in which the wind has been turned off
        for us to see exactly where the wind
            goes in and where it goes out

And here's the ON OFF button that turns the wind
    on and off, of course, and we don't turn it ON
        until we're OUT, and we watch the fans
            and bellows generate enough energy

And here's the middle of the generator
    where the power for the wind is stored
        when the wind isn't being used.
            Sir, don't press that ON button.

And now we'll leave the tunnel because very soon
    the owners will want to turn the wind on
        and watch things blow from one end of the tunnel
            to the other and back again.

DREAD

The cow is alone.
The other cow
dreads the pasture.

MUCH OBLIGED

My grandpa used to say "much obliged"
instead of "thank you"
when someone did him a favor.

He also used to tell me
when I was in a hurry,
"Take it easy, Greasy,
you got a long way to slide!"

When he died of throat cancer,
he banged his hand on the floor
to let everyone know it was happening.

At his wake, I half-expected, or hoped,
that he'd whisper to me
something like, "It's just like downtown,
only not so crowded!"

THIS IS TO SIGNIFY

that you, the reader
are aware that everything
going on around you
is made possible through the cooperation
of everybody, mind you, everybody,
who is involved, including
me and you, both of us.
Even though we might not be together,
we are here at the same moment
of time and space

on this very page, at this very point
in the power of language.
And you, the reader, are in control
of when and where we go
in your mind and the poem's.
You are the leader in this world.
I can only follow,
pushing for what it's worth.

EIGHTBALL

between the two
and the seven
lies the eightball
just waiting
         for the cue
ball to bash it
          into the corner pocket
or the side pocket
The cue ball
        caroms off the
              nine
and barely misses
        the eight
but the eightball rolls
into the nearest pocket
surprising all
        the other balls
including the eleven

ON THE DEATH OF W. H. AUDEN

I didn't know you died
till a week or so later
when Allan Kornblum told me
that he played your poetry record
at an open reading
at the Sanctuary, an Iowa City bar.
I made the posters
for that event, well-attended
I'm told, but I couldn't go
because I had bronchitis
and took antibiotics and codeine.
I heard you read in person
seven years ago at St. Louis U.'s gym.
That was the first poetry reading
I ever went to, and I was
deeply impressed, especially when
the microphone buzzed
and blew a fuse. You pushed it
away and angrily shouted,
DAMN THING! and everyone
thought that was funny,
but you were really pissed.
At this time I still don't know
how you died, or exactly when.
I'm sorry it happened
to you as well as Ezra
Pound, who died a few months ago,
and Pablo Neruda, who passed
away a few days before you.
I always pictured Pound
as a deposed monarch, Neruda
as a surrealistic king,
and you as a real, live poet.

* * * *from the* 1001 MARATHON POEMS * * *

CIRCUMNAVIGATE (602)

When the French say
    circumnavigate
they mean
    "How long it's been
        since we've met."

PROPERTY (667)

a long time ago
    everybody owned it

THEN: THUNDER (844)

    operating the sky
    i noticed
    how loud it was

PIE (850)

    destiny
    isolates
    the face

NEXT TO A GIRL (672)

the young boy
sat next to
a lamp

JOY FOREVER (675)

a thing of beauty
crashed to the floor

SYNTAX (705)

like a busted clock

APE (82)

dancing
        around

            the banana

APPLE

as a principle underlying the apple, the road
   contains nothing more than asphalt or cement

so we walk down the apple, figuring "this must
   be where a famous general walked and talked

about the new battle that would take place in
   the early hours of tomorrow morning."

the apple is beer. the drinkers of beer are
   satisfied with what it is, but no more than you

or I, or the tree on which the apple appears;
   lean back in the waves that the apple discharges

they make you feel as if you could think beyond
   the simple into the complex and then even further

THEY END IT

by turning to you
and saying
"That's all for now."